I0412975

WE, THE CHILDREN

The Hidden Language of Children

Victoria McGuinness

BALBOA.
PRESS
A DIVISION OF HAY HOUSE

Balboa Press books may be ordered through booksellers or by contacting:

Balboa Press
A Division of Hay House
1663 Liberty Drive
Bloomington, IN 47403
www.balboapress.com
1 (877) 407-4847

Print information available on the last page.

ISBN: 978-1-5043-4575-0 (sc)
ISBN: 978-1-5043-4576-7 (hc)
ISBN: 978-1-5043-4577-4 (e)

Library of Congress Control Number: 2015919094

Balboa Press rev. date: 04/01/2016

For my children Joya, Ben and Sue
applauding their courage.

Contents

Introduction

When my son, Ben, was four years old, he asked me, "Mama, when the new people come and the old ones leave, will they think of us as the Dark Ages?" I told my Gen X son that they might. Well, they are here.

This is a book applauding the new generations; this is a book inviting readers to reinvent the relationship they share with the children in their lives. This is a book for children's rights and about how we have left a planet hungry for regeneration to one of the most awesome generations to ever reach the earth. Since children are armed with an enormous amount of information and skill, their potential for helping or harming is intensified and multiplied. Their need and demand for connection and respect dominate daily life. As never before humans understand the tapestry of nature and nurture. Genetics may be 50 percent of our makeup and another 40 percent is our ability to empower ourselves and our children playing our best with the rest the cards we are dealt. We always feel better when we are the dealer. Woven together, this is our life.

The young people on the planet are built for the future in a way previous generations were not. Their difficult, brilliant, and confounding behaviors, vocabularies, sensitivities, and strengths are built in to survive in the unknowable and unimaginable world of 2030, 2035—you get the picture. It's difficult to understand a child's behavior today as related his or her need to survive in the future, but that is what we, the adults, need to do. Living in the absence of this new perspective can lead to apathy, depression even suicide.

Suicide is a major global public health problem, according to Seattle Children's Hospital and University of Washington, Medical School of Medicine. The new term is "self-directed violence," and it's on the rise worldwide.[1] Younger and younger children are obsessed with thoughts of dying or being killed. Even when my Gen X kids were children, suicide didn't appear on their radar as an option to get out of life or to solve problems. Suicide in very young children is generally not recognized as such, but some kids ride their bikes into traffic or run out into the street, drink poison, or find an unguarded gun and use it. Of course, very young kids might say "I wish I was dead; I want to kill myself" to finally get their parents' or teachers' attention, but it's disturbing that such young children are making these statements more frequently and that older children are engaging in self-directed violence and death by suicide. This sad truth invites adults everywhere to use some god glue when it comes to connecting with kids. God-glue attaches the child and the adult like super-glue; never let go of the soul connection by letting them know we're all in this together. This is accomplished by gluing your eyes on a child in a kind, loving and understanding way and spending time with them. I call this connection our god-glue.

This book took many years of experience to write. As much as this book is a professional work, writing it has required the weaving together of the constant thread of my own spiritual journey with my work. True and sacred psychology seeks to integrate spirituality with clinical knowledge; life either has meaning, or it doesn't. Intensely being with children in their world for the past twenty-five years has helped to heal my childhood wounds by opening my heart and expanding my understanding of the many facets of being human. Play therapy allows child to experience a whole-hearted integration of their weaknesses and their strengths, their traumas and triumphs. I'm truly blessed to be able to give and receive healing simultaneously; in truth, giving and receiving are the same energy, and I have been blessed with the experience over and over again through work and play.

Parents who seek guidance and understanding have asked me to write about how young children communicate through metaphor and association. This book reveals the inner world of childhood as created in experiential play therapy by the children. The book includes some personal childhood stories that provide the living section of my credentials. I have been a therapist for exactly one half of my life; I have absorbed thousands of stories like most long-working therapists. Through witnessing the power of play therapy, I have learned to respect my own journey and feel that the playroom has brought me the power to transform my own (sad) story while facilitating healing and growth in others. And now, my story is only sad if I agree to that. The gift my parents gave me is the ability to not only survive in adversity but to thrive – a gift for which I say thank-you every day.

We, the Children offers a glimpse into just a handful of children's stories out of the thousands of children's journeys I've had life-changing opportunities to witness and support. Years have gone into writing and revising this work, from focusing exclusively on parenting to bringing a message that invites all loving adults to consider the living truth of a child's play as well as the play's reliability and accuracy in revealing that personal truth.

At some point, a writer has to abandon the work; it is never finished, never complete, especially these days as time races by in a blur and the world seems to be changing very fast. Every day so many people feel like they have no time when the same twenty-four hours still tick away. Again, this book is meant to be an invitation for adults to move even one degree closer to the child or children in their lives or to reach out to new little ones. A spiritual revolution stirs in the belly of humanity as we see the planetary legacy we have left to our children. One way to further this spiritual revolution is to connect deeply with the littles you come into relationship with heart-to-heart. This new and youngest generation as a whole has clearly demonstrated that children's behavior cannot be controlled. We can motivate healing in our children and ourselves by connecting spirit to spirit. This means changing our perceptions of adult and child relationships, especially in the area of power and control. Adults can minimize these emotionally charged issues by teaching negotiation and cooperation lowering everyone's stress. In the playroom, sword fights often represent issues of power and control. Most children feel the need to put armor for protection. In childhood, this armor protects us; as adults it harms us.

Back in 2003, a parent wrote to me about just such a connection with her foster child. Although the child wrote his letters upside down and backward, he had just assembled a very complicated cardboard toy from Chuck E. Cheese's.

> When he got them, I took one look at the little pieces and knew it was hopeless, way too complicated—that we'd have to get someone else to help. He had two sets of motorcycle pieces. He was quiet for a while and then walked into my room, carrying two perfectly assembled, tiny motorcycles like two rare butterflies. He looked me right in the eye, because he knew I was going to be amazed. I *was* amazed. Truly. He'd done something very difficult and done it perfectly, and he knew it. He was inside the light of his heart. It's hard to describe, but something happened at that moment. I felt very connected to him, with him looking right at me with those blue eyes, knowing he'd done something significant. As

> he left the room, he turned around and said: "I love you."
>
> I've wondered so much about whether our relationship has an impact—and a moment like this makes me know that it does, for him and for me. And that it's about spirit more than anything. All the rest is necessary to prepare the way, the bare necessities maybe, but a moment like this is where the growth happens, for me and for him, in a big leap. It's odd how something like that feels like a meeting of pure spirit, like he's not younger (or poorer) than I am, that we were meeting just as ourselves, on the level ground of love.[2]

Once I was told by a reputable hand-reader that I was in the School of Love in this life – that I came to learn about love. Playing with children has provided various and fascinating assignments: although I have not graduated, I have glimpsed the inner workings of today's child helping me to cultivate a love of humanity and the need to re-define what it means to be human. Biology is no longer destiny. Consider just the gender revolution of the millennial children.

The following provides a tiny glimpse into the social plight of a transgender child.

One day, I was on my knees in the waiting room with Stevie. We were waiting for Stevie's mother to return after her session. A rather conservative and well-meaning woman was also sitting in the waiting room while her child gathered her belongings. Now, I knew from playing with Stevie on and off for the past two years that she didn't like to be told she was pretty; that remark was a trigger for her. She was transgender and had been struggling with this awareness since she was a toddler and discovered a misplaced penis. The woman said to Stevie, "You are so pretty!"

I felt Stevie's eyes click into mine; there was a slight jerk of her abundant black curls—how to play the role with an adult who assumes she is a girl because she looks like a girl not knowing that she is a girl in a boy's body? She sought my eyes for support and connection before answering the questions. Then the woman said, "Your hair is so beautiful too!" Another click—maybe she thought of how she plays about camouflage in the playroom—working out her need for disguises. This was a common theme in Stevie's play. She said, eyes shifting over to mine, relishing our connection, the silent validation and encouragement all at once, "I made it that way! I cut it off, and it grew back curly." Stevie flashed her winning smile just as her mother returned to pick her up. She is like light—brilliant and perhaps an ancient two-spirited soul. Indigenous cultures recognized tribal members who identified with both the male and female gender as created as a third gender. We don't know yet how to fully comprehend or respect this gender variance. What we do know is that childhood has never looked like this; a simple two-gender option no longer fits. And we all know the price of assumptions.

CHAPTER ONE

We, the Children

We, the children … are as vulnerable as we are strong, as ignorant as we are wise, as powerful as we are powerless, as naughty as we are nice, and as angry as we are sweet. We, the children, are here to help save and serve the world but also need the world to serve and save us. We are you embracing and expressing all of what humanity has become. We are here to remind you that what is done to children is done to everyone, everywhere. Look around. We are reaping what you have sown, and we, the children, are not pleased. We have been described as the Indigo Children, the Psychic Ones; we have been over-diagnosed with disorders, at times governed by too much medication. We are suffocating from too much information, too many rules, not enough nature—absorbing too many violent images, including many reflecting a very fragile future no matter where we live. Because we are losing our innocence sooner, experiencing the end of childhood sooner than any previous generations, we need to connect with you as spiritual equals. We are the creative problem solvers, and you need our help; we are psychic, brilliant, sensitive, callous, defiant, and demanding. You have to earn our respect; it is no longer a given.*

Entering into a child's world through play or other child-oriented actions is one way to communicate respect for the young child's plight on the planet and thereby gain more respect for adults in general.

Play therapy is easily very supportive of children and has a long history. Rousseau (1930–1962) wrote that learning about children by watching their play helps people understand them better. In the early 1900s, Anna Freud used small toys and sand trays to diagnose young children and help children reveal feelings from the inside out. Play is both ancient and universal, but for some reason, the tendency to discount play as meaningful prevails. Dismissing child's play as merely that—child's play and therefore trivial—continues as a form of prejudice against their language. Because children are denied a voice, there are times when their rights are severely denied, dismissed, and deemed unimportant.

This is a book about integrating early childhood communication, play therapy, systems, and the generally invisible dimensions of our beings. In the 1940s, Dr. Virginia Mae Axline, PhD, wrote *Dibs in Search of Self*, one of the first books that revealed the genius and power of play therapy. Dibs's wealthy parents had brought him to Virginia, a clinical psychologist, for therapy under the dark cloud of shame. At five years old, he wasn't talking or playing with his peers. Instead, Dibs hid for hours behind a couch or inside a closet. Believing their son to be "retarded" (in the vernacular of the day), his parents took him to play therapy with Virginia.

To make a long story short, the adults discovered that Dibs was, in fact, a genius who had been reading volumes behind the couch or inside the closet to avoid his cold and rejecting mother and virtually absent father, a live-from-the-neck-up money-making machine. Imagine their surprise as the truth of their child's genius was actually quite the opposite truth of what they believed. It is important to note that back in 1947, Dr. Axline felt that children were hurried and rushed in life; they were out of sync with their naturally slower pace—they needed time to absorb and integrate experiences. Need I say more?[1]

In 2016, children are simply unable to keep up with the information overload they are almost constantly exposed to. Talk about rushing development. Humans clearly appear to have evolved to survive, at least cognitively — human emotional and spiritual development is not this fast. More than ever before, children need time to process in order to find balance between their brilliance with the fact that they are still children both attracted and repelled to the lure and the pressure of too much information.

This is a book of true stories contained in the metaphors children have created, one as young as twenty-three months. Toys expand a child's vocabulary, allowing a full-body expression of feelings and experiences. This expression allows for more positive thoughts and actions. The purpose of therapeutic play provides a way for children to master their internal and external reality, both positive and negative. New research indicates that play enhances the child-brain's ability to create new neuro-pathways, increase oxytocin levels and activate mirror neurons. This download of positivity helps children to more easily connect with adults and also to better imitate adults for better or worse for real or in delusion.

People use fantasy to survive difficult situations or enhance pleasant ones. This is the true purpose most fantasy play provides in the playroom – a sort of oblivion. When fantasy or make-believe is involved it serves as a protection against the realities of life and growing up. Fantasy provides a sort of magic activated by play that helps children to grow naturally in empathy, imitation and understanding.

But in the inner reality, for example, what appear to be fantasy such as labeling "bad guys" can symbolize for the child their negative thoughts and feelings, maybe about other people or about themselves; either way, the content of this play contains real projections of each child's experiences as he or she works to master them. Play therapy provides children with the opportunity to engage deeply in emotional work in accordance with their developmental and emotional level of processing regardless of their age that produces self-affirming behavior from the inside out. [2]

Ultimately, this book isn't a scientific work but a work of the heart I generated after witnessing close to twenty-five hundred soul journeys young children shared in a therapeutic playroom. I prefer the term soul journeys to case studies. There, children's natural storytelling abilities are enhanced because they don't always need to use words to communicate.

One of the youngest children to regain developmental mastery over this stage of her life was the daughter of divorcing medical doctors; she was twenty-three months old. Maya's mother had brought her to therapy to see why she wouldn't eat or sleep at day care. Maya's mother had a busy medical practice, and Maya was losing weight and her mother was loosing sleep. They had reached a critical point in life.

Within just a few sessions, Maya set up a table and chairs in the dollhouse and chose a gray-haired doll to represent the adult, whom she showed pacing around the children in the chairs. Then she tossed the older woman out the playhouse window. Maya repeated this play over and over in that session, so I asked her mother who was in charge of giving the children their snacks and supervising naptime. Her mother told me it was an older woman.

"Does she have gray hair?" I asked. Affirmative. I said, "Well, Maya doesn't like her."

Much to the mother's surprise, Maya was less upset about the divorce than about the day care woman she didn't like. After a suggestion that someone else should serve the meals and supervise napping, Maya ate and slept, and her mother recovered from her exhaustion.

This is a book about knowing versus perception; this knowing is a marriage of intellect and heart. Ultimately, intellect is the triumph of the ego, and in these days of ego dominance, the longings and needs of our collective spiritual hearts are being silenced. Although the human ego needs nurturance and connection to blossom into balance and health possessing positive human traits; a damaged or maladaptive ego leads to selfishness or violence and other negative human traits. Some quite horrific as we have observed throughout history. Children contain the natural push toward healing and empowering themselves; adults need reminders. This is a book of reminders of what it means to be human—and of what we know viscerally without external proof. It seems time to extend our understanding of what it means to be human. We contain both the darkness and the light of humanity. As children, we may not have a choice, but as adults we do and the darkness cannot exist in the light. We are both. We've made a mistake to try and eradicate our darker natures and increase their strength by denying this half of ourselves. Integration of the duality leads to kindness and compassion; accepting we are both is the key to redefining what it means to be fully human.

Although I'm a fan of scientific research and applaud myself when science validates my ideas, beliefs influence even the most objective of researchers and scientists—most importantly, their *unconscious* beliefs. The parts of our lives that aren't working or aren't satisfying reflect the inner power of the unconscious to influence our lives by disrupting the illusion of control we have over our own feelings and behaviors. The symbols of our physical lives represent the deeper meanings and influences of our inner worlds. The power of the unconscious is unstoppable. For example, adults who lost their parents to death when they were children find their own children experiencing the same loss in their childhood. We are seemingly powerless over the projection of what lies deep inside us that seeks to manifest outwardly. Do you ever suddenly feel as if you married your mother or father? Or you discover a new aspect of your partner's personality or lifestyle that had been hidden from you and suddenly, you are partnered with a stranger. That's the unconscious in action. In a therapeutic playroom, children's play naturally encompasses both conscious and unconscious material – this way, it is revealed.

Remembering the language of childhood—the intensity and depth of children's feelings, the impact of early imprinting on learning and brain formation motivated by innate curiosity, and the magical world of nature—provides a bridge between what is passing and what is coming for adult-child relationships. Now, in the twenty-first century, more than ever, remembering and honoring what it's like to be someone's beloved child or someone's inconvenience, to be an mere extension of a parent's ego or self-absorption, to provide a whipping post, or to live any other childhood experience is an important part of assisting in global healing or a better kind of global warming. The world we have bequeathed to our children requires that we bridge the generational gap with love. The power of all children's stories is to bridge a vital connection between adults and children as the world shifts on its axis, both literally and metaphorically. If we were truly created because God loves stories, then we haven't disappointed the power of all that is, call that life-force God, Allah, Buddha or Jesus – call it energy, call it vibrating molecules. What ever you label "it" – honor It.

Although *We, the Children* isn't research heavy, there is plenty of concrete research to support its message, particularly on the subject of the value and power of play therapy. I cannot resist the urge to say that the reference section at the end of this book is as complete as I could get it to be. I suppose one of the effects of my childhood is to be a curmudgeon in certain areas. Because I decided to rewrite the research and statistics sections of the book instead of asking for permission to use copyrighted material (even if posted on the Internet), the lack of supporting evidence for the assertions in this book may be apparent. Being an avid reader myself, I enjoy a direct message from the author, so I took this risk of being less intellectual and more feelings based. However, there is a lot of new research to support the importance of play for everyone!

The concept that our intellect is all we need helps to support the illusion that we have control over a vast and unknowable universe. But Mother Nature often reminds us that this belief just isn't so, often in the shape of a screaming toddler and other human storms.

Research and statistics have an essential place in our world, but frankly, data can be used to prove or disprove just about anything, and all data is flawed. Intellect and technology have done as much harm to humans as they have helped taking away time better spent nourishing our hearts and souls. When children play about this kind of loss, they almost always choose a robber as a metaphoric character. Children know when they are being robbed of something they need: a relationship or a certain type of nurturing or experience. Have we robbed them of a sustainable place to live? Of clean food to eat? Have we robbed them of deep human connections? Are we all being programmed to allow our phones, rather than our inner knowing, to control us? I can tell you the answer is still out there somewhere. We are an X-file, maybe the most mysterious case ever.

Watching the news, we see only the outer form of a person; people are black, white, gay, straight, trans, male, female, and so on. We are blind to seeing the *content* of a person's character or soul, and adults need to open their spiritual eyes and teach the facts of our shared humanness to children beyond form.

Increasingly, the same argument is used to support two totally divergent points of view. For example, the saying "God doesn't make mistakes" justifies both that gay and trans people are sinners and that they are just being who they are. The age-old justification for violent religious wars is that "God is on *our side*," which somehow justifies murder in the name of God; oddly, everyone believes he or she (or the group) is the chosen. Maybe we all are chosen if we choose to be.

Simply put, the children's stories are a departure from pure intellectualism from the neck up. Experiencing and knowing are intertwined and the outcome of anyone's experience combined with their awareness makes the outcome unpredictable. This is a personal and universal truth. Many adults who are strongly biased against their own children's preferences or expressions overcome this bias only by discovering the *content* of their own children's true inner natures. It is by knowing a person's inner being that we can eradicate prejudice and hate, but as the world spins, we don't seem to have time for this. Physics reveals new data, flawed or not, that supports the notion that visualization and imagination create reality. Science is still catching up with the idea that showing kids how to envision how things can be, or how they want themselves to be, will increase their chances of achieving their goals such as surviving or thriving in spite of their parent's divorce. Adapting to two homes is becoming the norm. All I can say is that most Parenting Plans give me a raging headache. The adjustments and expectations we have of children these days is all mixed up. We might demand they adjust to two homes where everything is completely different, the bed, the food, the rules, the pets, the people, the bathtub, but don't expect them to learn self-reliance, communication and support by providing those lessons during and after a divorce.

Divorce used to be a shocking event, but as beliefs change over time divorce is emerging as a new normal, or the new abnormal, if you like. Social constructs we've held near and sacred, such as marriage and gender are still dear and considered sacred. It's who gets to engage in or extend these socially constructed institutions that appears to be an issue. Finding out what is good for humans or not apparently fluctuates dramatically over time.

It took scientist fifty years to prove that breast milk is better for babies than formula. To seek evidence is necessary, I suppose, but feeding your baby a manufactured formula, unless medically necessary, is an example of a thought system propelled by the ego in the world. Clearly it's becoming more impossible to decide what is good to eat, think, drink, and so on, because the evidence keeps changing. Advancing from superstition and mythologies to what we can see and touch as reality, humanity sought truth through science. Now the pendulum has swung too far into a so-called rational thought system that isn't really rational at all as evidenced by the depleted state of our earth and the horrors of racial and religious relations. Just about anyone with eyes can see that in spite of the efforts of many, who keep trying to heal the separations created by age, skin color, sexual preferences, gender fluidity and so on, we are in worse shape than ever. There are just too many humans on earth for us to be violent or aggressive; it's like a wildfire that catches and burns. When the pendulum swings back, the human heart might just be sliced in half, as we realize it may be too late to save the seven seas from pollution. We've created a mess from sea to not so shining sea and handed it over to the children.

The body or ego and the spirit of the human soul don't share the same thought system and are, in fact, opposite. The rise in popularity of yoga, mindfulness and other practices to integrate and calm the mind and body may be pointing to our need to reconcile duality; body and soul, mind and brain, ego and spirit to survive this intense time of transition. The children need our help to calm down, trust and integrate. Their behavior will force adults to calm down, trust and integrate or go crazy. Pressure to grow spiritually.

Children seem to come straight from heaven (or occasionally from hell). Either way, it takes time for children to be domesticated and programmed into the thought system of the world. As human beings, we seem to enter the world in a state of grace and wisdom. As babies, our communication is clear. We cry when in distress, we smile when pleased. Infants are masters of non-verbal and non-violent communication designed to facilitate survival. Infants and children are easy prey; they have no ultimate power. Even so, adults are astounded by what very small toddlers can be capable of with their little fingers flying over keyboards and phones. The children's need for control is rising as our lives spin out of control.

These days the pre-K children can be as controlling as past generations were in middle school or high school. Programming for social competition appears to be happening to children at much younger ages and faster than their minds and bodies can keep up with. Kids are exposed to information overload, stimulation overload and the need for perfection. The bombarding of our children with information adds unprecedented challenges to normal development, and these days, it's like trying to stop a speeding bullet. Mindfulness is the key that unlocks the door of prevention. The children are the culmination of humankind; they need calm aware adults at their side to guide them. It's time to wake up and get real; stop teaching children that things define who they are.

I wonder if Erick Erickson's psychosocial stages of development (1950, 1963) will have to be revised to suit the new ones.[3] Children are certainly doing things sooner and faster and rather competently. The stages of healthy human development must occur in order to preserve our species; the planet will survive but will we?

> Infancy: Able to communicate needs expertly—The true task of Infancy is to establish an inner climate of trust instead of mistrust fostering a sense of hope about being human and cared for. Erickson viewed hope as a basic human virtue developed in Infancy or the first fourteen or fifteen months of life. Adults need to securely attach to their infant because the millennial

generations are becoming known for their lack of trust.

Toddler: Can operate Xbox, the Wii, your phone, etc. So how distracting are these additional tasks? Since this is a time to build a brain that is autonomous and actively engaged in life with a strong but flexible will or ego? How hard is it to outsmart a two or three year old child?

These are simply questions to consider the main one being how does a constant interface with technology shape a child's sense of self, their relationships and the social construction of their world? How does this interface change the directions of a wonderfully plastic and adaptable brain? How do we balance nature, nurture, and now electronics are surely a big part of the mix.

One threat to be aware of is the feeling of competition children feel when one of their peers nets five million from a U-tube video or an idea that takes off. Geez! Should I just go get a job? (No way!) Work?

This type of U-tube luck can lead to the years of identity confusion as an adolescent (which is now defined as the second-dozen years, or twelve to twenty-five). One of the most significant gifts adults can bestow upon the youngest generation is to redirect the emphasis on competition into a race to see who can best serve the needs of our planet.

The not so old programming that informed us that everyone should and can get a college education, get a job, obtain a house, and find an opposite-gender spouse is a myth lashed to the backs of the Gen Xers and millennial kids in a way that differs from previous generations. Achieving these goals is less and less possible without a ton of support and soon without a ton of money. Video games and Apps provide the perfect escape from reality often merging in a confused heap in the mind of a young child.

I know for a fact that young children who are exposed to violent video games and movies can't handle the aftermath of the haunting images. The *images* are too powerful, and even if they appear to be fine during the day, they may become extremely frightened at night because the images once seen are not easily forgotten. Does it follow, then, that being aware of competition for resources, water, food, dying species of animals, cruelty among people, or income inequality will actually motivate children to strive to create a better self and a happy future? I can tell you that this awareness is a double-edged sword, igniting either the flame of selfishness and an extreme need to feel in control and acquire the latest and greatest thing or a who-cares and why-bother attitude.

The forecast states that by 2016 the richest 1 percent will control more wealth than the bottom 99 percent.[4] If I think this is a chilling economic forecast, I think I'd feel a lot worse if I were younger with more possible future in front of me. I've observed that the new kids won't tolerate being robbed of their rights without one heck of a fight—and an extremely intelligent fight armed with technological skill perhaps imparting an upper hand? Historically the 1 percent has always been in power, while we peasants scrape for basics. Maybe the new kids will help to change that. World population just cannot sustain the old system any longer. A new paradigm arises and, with it, a new world order. We are experiencing the shift now, even if we cannot know what is coming. I bring these seemingly unrelated issues up because they are all related to the anxiety and violence children have to endure, giving rise to their obsession with death.

When it comes to relating to children, always ask, "What am I teaching?" Children are more likely to learn what you are *not consciously trying to teach them.* Perfect examples are yelling and spanking; these actions teach children to yell and hit. Children learn from your innermost motivations and fears; children learn by the behavior you model and from the way they are treated. What adults say almost doesn't matter. This new generation's response to harsh discipline mimics dolphin behavior; dolphins don't respond to negative reinforcement or punishment, instead they will swim away to the bottom of the tank or pool and ignore any instructions based on punishment—and so it is with the new kids. Adult dolphins stay very close to their young and raise them in a pod often playing leaf-tag with them. I think there is something to learn from them.

As more and more children in the Western world are allowed creative avenues of expression, we will find all their struggles with duality of being human reflected in their stories. We know the power of our childhood stories in shaping the rest of our lives. In experiential play therapy, the child is invited to share his or her story any way he or she wants to as long as it's safe. Experiential play therapy has the power to transform potentially harmful, scary stories and memories, negative feelings, and self-concepts into new and truer stories so we can remember who we are and, more importantly, *live out of that inner knowing.*

I know I survived my early childhood experiences in part, because I could go out and play. Remember Dibs was spared a life of torture through one adult's willingness to get down on the floor and play with him. Truly communicating and revealing the truth of this child's genius, how he protected himself through isolation and self-education, demonstrates the power of connecting with children at their level—not merely as children but as spiritual equals. Infants are little gurus fresh from home.

When truly communicating with a child through play, we encounter a kind of living communication that is fresh and true. *We, the Children* invites the reader to consider the meaning of children's uncontaminated play themes and how this shift in perspective further invites a new dialogue regarding children's rights. We can then reevaluate the measure to which their voices are heard in the legal system, educational system, and other systems.

The younger the child, the more pure the communication; but this requires revisiting and remembering our first language. *A Course in Miracles (ACIM)* teaches that the body is a communication device,[5] so it follows that young children, not having oral language readily available to them, are masters of symbolic language and nonverbal communication. Nonverbal communication conveys 65 to 85 percent of a message; therefore, so much communication is lost when one meets someone only in cyberspace. Is this lack of physicality a symbol of our personal isolation? Of the walls we erect through technology in our relationships? Are these reflective of our need for inner space? Or are "others" a mirror neuron reflecting something about humanity we refuse to view directly?

Metaphors and symbols are everywhere—in all of life, reflecting ourselves back to ourselves. The emergence of the iPhone—the "i" everything—is certainly a metaphor for our times, reflecting the adoration and centrality of the ego at the almost total expense and disregard of community locally and globally. Too much focus on Selfie!

Speaking up for the rights of children in the Western world where, relatively speaking, they are given glorious lives compared to the complete disregard of childhood needs experienced in many places around the globe. But I learned a long time ago not to compare people's pain. Children everywhere need this shift in adult consciousness and connection with their adult community.

America's millennial children need to be heard when decisions regarding their lives are on the table. A time of reconsidering our thoughts, words, and deeds is called for, no matter where we live and what we think. We need to envision a viable and sustainable future for the children, who are the foundation of the future for everyone. But the old guard, who are still clinging on, frustratingly control us through media and money. More and more regular folks wake up to a feeling of powerlessness as the rich get richer and we scrape by in protest, asking, "Who are these people?" We all know the future world is a huge deal our children are facing. We teach them that money and acquisition are power, perhaps forgetting the truth of true personal empowerment. The voices of the youngest generations will be broadcast through the media because they know how to do it. At least, I hope so.

I thought I gave up wanting to know why. But now, at sixty-five, I'm like a three-year-old again and really wish I could truly know why things happen.

For example, the debate over whether a zygote has rights may not be as important as changing legislation regarding adoption and children's right for a family who wants them. Let's consider the rights of a five-year-old, whom the loving foster family he or she is living with (and can't legally snuggle with) can't adopt because his or her absent biological parent, who does nothing for the child, clings to "parental rights" over the child he or she hasn't legally relinquished. Being adopted at any age comes with issues, but there are considerably fewer issues at one and a half or two than at six, seven, or beyond. So far, parental rights surpass the rights of children in the eyes of the law in abandonment cases. This is another item that needs to be reviewed more fairly, with an open mind to the wellbeing of the child, and changed to consider the rights of the abandoned child.

I have gotten numerous calls from parents of children, whom the other parents abandoned for years. The absent parent now wants access to his or her child and has the nerve to ask for 50 percent custody, including visitation every other weekend, even though he or she has been missing for half of the child's life. Parents who harm and abandon their children are granted parental rights for far too long, denying children the right to become part of a new family who wants them.

Another dilemma concerning the rights of children versus the rights of parents who don't keep their children is open adoption. Frankly, this arrangement doesn't work for young children and appears to serve the needs of the adults, not those of the kids. Every child I have known who has been in someone's guardianship or whom another family has adopted and is mandated to have visits with the birth parent or parents is tortured by these meetings. This is like ripping the proverbial Band-Aid off an unhealed wound, causing emotional anguish for the child. When a person reaches a reasonable age in his or her teen years or beyond and *chooses* to meet his or her birth parents, that is a choice he or she can make on his or her own.

The world is brimming with causes and cases—just about everyone except the ruling class is fighting for basic human rights. This one is for the typical kid, the mega-millennial who, in just over a decade, will be an extremely influential part challenging the ruling class. Underestimating children is something we've done for ages while simultaneously expecting them to act like small adults. We just got that one all wrong. Sometimes, children do act like adults.

When five-year-old Jewel (of *The Broken Truth her words are on the back cover of this book*) put her hands on her hips, shook her red curls, and stomped around the playroom, exclaiming, "My attorney says I can't go visit my father in Hawaii until I'm at least seven-years-old. I am so mad at my attorney," this gives one pause. Yes, adults do need to make decisions for children; adults need to fully consider the desires and rights of the child for balance in decision-making.

So, if you're on board with re-entering the world of childhood, I wanted to share the perfect haiku written by a friend of mine that captures the essence of play therapy:

I need to play, cry,
Push toy dump trucks through the pain,
Hauling off my tears.
Turinni 2013

The teller of stories has power over us, because we have faith in his or her story. Faith isn't cognitive—it is the power of the heart to join with the storyteller.

Carl Jung said that the unconscious is the key to life's pursuits. Jung engaged in building sand tray stories of his own childhood to understand his history and discover what was hidden in his unconscious mind. We encounter the power of the programming that lies beneath the surface of our awareness, when our behaviors surprise or horrify us. For example: "I wasn't going to say that. I wasn't going to eat that. I didn't know I felt so angry or sad. I said I'd never cheat on my spouse or spank my children and yada yada." The drive from our unconscious creates confounding behavior out of its nature to express. This is sort of like having a ghost driving the bus.

The content of the unconscious manifests everywhere in our lives, and if we but start to see the messages written in the invisible ink of other dimensions, we can heal our lives. The best use of time may indeed be to create and heal, not to spend all our energies and resources acquiring the most toys, because only what is created and healed within goes with us when we depart from this mortal coil. (I can say this because of an NDE (near-death experience) I had in 2002, the countless dearly departed souls I know, and the hundreds of "paranormal" experiences I've had and read about.) We don't get to take our toys, but we do take our internal experiences and choices with us.

As a young child, I identified with black people and felt the pain of being totally misunderstood. When I was five years old, I sat alone in the basement, weeping as I watched *Uncle Tom's Cabin.* My mother was a bigot; I'm unclear as to my father's position on race. I wept as a child while witnessing the incomprehensible relationship between blacks and whites, patriarchal authority, and the rest of us. When I was ten, I read *Black like Me*, a story about a white man who pretended to be black to see what it felt like.

Of course, I was an anathema to my mother, but our relationship was much more insidious than that. Until recently, I wouldn't have lumped our prejudice against children into a mess of prejudice against people—whites against blacks, people of "color" against us whites, people in authority against the powerless—but now I do.

Has a generational gap lead to a surge regarding the importance of play for children? Is there too much emphasis on testing and scores and not enough focus on teaching children to shape their own brains through play and brain training? What we don't want is the problem of adults against children. This is a worn-out theme in human history. Children whose lives consist of missed opportunities to play and imagine grow up to be very troubled adults.

Sean

Play is essential for human development, and it is through playing that children think about adult-type things in childlike ways. I met a four-year-old, Sean, who had an imaginary friend named Gallop. He said to me while riding Gallop, "Babies first—it's the dawn of a new race."

The child who rode Gallop called family meetings *on his own* and led them. Sean was clearly more evolved than his parents. Imagine a tyke of a mere four years old calling a family meeting in their living room and asking his mother to "speak first." Sean informed his family, "We have to talk about these things." He told his parents that he was afraid of the dark and needed to sleep with his mother. He applauded his father when the suggestion was made that his father actually come home for dinner and eat with the family. Sean also told the family that they needed to talk about fear the family felt. Sean wasn't satisfied with the nurturing his parents were giving him and clearly took control of his upbringing. This same little boy couldn't stop pestering his mother about the difference between a video store and a movie theater (this was back in the nineties). In one session, Sean built a machine to "tear away the skin of cute girls because of the feelings they give me."

The point is that the new kids can express extremely complex, conflicting human feelings through play. Sean also watched the entire 9/11 footage on the news. He insisted, "I have to know what's happening." Yes, 9/11 unnerved the world and rocked the playroom. His fears helped him and his father grow emotionally closer. Sean is just another perfect example of a highly evolved human being; he led the way to his family's healing through his own initiative and his own experience in the playroom.

CHAPTER TWO

A Crash Course in Experiential Play Therapy; Norton's Model and Beyond

This will be as brief and clear an explanation as I can provide about a complex interaction between a child, the playroom, the therapist and the parent(s) and the world. (Reading about play and communicating with little ones isn't as interesting as actually being engaged with a child.) The basic structure of forming a meaningful relationship with a young child through play builds the foundation of therapy, parenting, interviewing, teaching, training, and so on. If you think of the playroom as a metaphor for life and the stages as a reflection of the developmental stages of most humans in the world navigate defining relationship with others.

Three Basic Elements

1. Young children communicate primarily through metaphor and association, mood and behavior, in a mostly nonverbal world swirling with images, sensations, sounds, textures, and feelings. The human brain absorbs

and records every single word, nuance, and event it experiences, creating neurological pathways in the brain that are either healthy or twisted. Later these are called "implicit" or "unconscious/cellular" memories.

2. Children are always communicating; not always non-verbally, the new ones can be quite articulate.
3. Children's play is meaningful.

When a child enters the playroom for the first time, the "exploratory stage" initiates the relationship. Children either explore the toys or stand anxiously aside, exploring with their eyes. Some children BOOM into their play and begin. I like to call this stage the "discovery stage," especially with these new kids, because they seem to be all about discovering what's in the room, what their interests are and who you are while they explore. They encounter their deepest feelings while seeking safety in their discoveries and self-expression.

Simultaneously and throughout therapy, children test the therapist for emotional safety or protection. Children want to know we can handle their emotions and still like them, even though they hit their little sister sometimes or carry the shame of their abuse.

This generation exceeds anyone's expectations and wildest dreams regarding their ability to test adults for their ability to provide safety, healthy boundaries, set limits and understanding as well as respectful guidance. The establishment of trust takes time for most kids, but this really depends on their prior experiences and conditioning. Some kids know right away that the playroom is a safe place; others take much longer to realize this.

The "working and processing stage" is hard and requires commitment from everyone involved in the child's life including the child. The stories in this book primarily illustrate the working stage of therapy I like to call the "processing stage." The amazing thing about this model, which most play therapy models don't allow for, is the *redoing* of tattered, unfinished, traumatic stages of development and the rewiring of the brain with new and more positive pathways by enhancing neurological plasticity and growth.

Processing trauma that happened at two years old when one is five is challenging, but most children have a knack for this type of healing and also know within seconds what the playroom is for—what it offers them in its colorful neutrality. It's a place where for an hour a week there is no judgment, either good or bad. No one tells the child what to do; there's just some adult who reflects back to the child his or her beauty, intelligence, struggles, and strengths.

Parents and kids need support to process. This stage is a treasure for those who really want to know the truth of a child's experience. For example, what did the child experience with an alleged perpetrator? Within this stage of play adults may find the answers. They find not only the answers but their child's inner truth by believing his or her story.

After "redoing" a messed-up or disrupted developmental stage their way with adult support, children move into the "growth stage" and experience a reconnection with their original selves as well as with their caretakers at the deepest level possible for them at this stage. The relief children experience in this stage is enormous, not to mention the utter relief of parents (and the therapist.) We all enjoy the developmental leap that ensues after much hard work. I like to call this stage "learning and living the lessons stage."

"Saying good-bye" is the final stage of the experiential model. This is again rather particular to the child and family's situation as well as the child's bonding and attachment experiences. Given the freedom to complete a course of therapy, saying good-bye is like good friends having to part. Ideally, this is a planned event over a course of a number of sessions, in which the issue of separation is addressed as well as the celebration of the renewed sense and restoration of the child's truest self and ability to journey through the next stages of development.[1]

I will always be grateful to Dr. Norton for his creation of experiential play therapy, because this model facilitates healing not only for children everywhere but also for the therapist and other adults in the child's life.[2]

The Magic of Metaphors

The human unconscious is a metaphor-making machine. For example, Gracie, my sister's grandchild, was only four when she exclaimed, "I'm gonna throw you under the bus, Gran'ma." And that meant telling on my sister to my niece. Gracie fully understood the concept behind the thought at four years old and tried to use it to get her way. Light-hearted Bonnie, a preschool child shopping for new boots, told the salesman she needed boots "in size pink, please," knowing exactly how she envisioned herself wearing them. Familiar phrases such as "pushing the envelope" or "cutting the mustard," "chewing on ideas," "digesting events and conversations," "boiling with anger," "burning with love," "smoldering with rage," "floating on air," and so on convey feelings and ideas most people quickly understand. Simply put, the use of metaphor is a way of describing something by comparing it to something else. On a very basic level, *meta* means "across," and *phor* means to "carry or carry across."

Children are geniuses in their ability to transfer their emotions, perceptions, and experiences to tangible forms, such as sand, art, and toys through highly metaphoric or symbolic play language. This can then be translated for the curious or concerned adult. So often, simply observing and verbalizing a child's play as it unfolds reveals in language the connection between the child's inner world of images into clear communication that bridges the relationship between the child and the adult. So sometimes just saying what they're playing spells things out. For example, most children with separation anxiety or loss issues bury things in the sand.

Reflecting the loss, I might say, "Oh, that one disappeared. We can't see that one right now they are missing." And without the child using language, we communicate at the deepest level a true sense of separation or loss. Children live in the world of metaphors; it swarms with pictures, sensations, textures, sounds, smells, ghosts, and bogeymen. It is replete with dragons, fairies, and monsters.

Almost all children experience five predictable stages of experiential play therapy as described above. The way a child explores and discovers, tests and finds trust, works by processing and integrating material, progresses and leaves the experience is the way the child approaches and interacts with his or her life and the people in his or her life. Thousands of children have had the experience of replaying and healing trauma, abandonment, abuse, divorce, adoption, and other childhood pressures in playrooms throughout the United States and Europe. Stories, parables, and metaphors are the best teachers, as so many spiritual masters and teachers have demonstrated. Children tell their stories in the language of play, and the light metaphors shed on inner truth.

We believe the storyteller, who holds us in his or her power during the telling. When children have the opportunity to tell their stories of victimization as children, they can let go and transform into the identity of victor and not carry the victim mentality for the next ten, twenty, or more years. This change creates a fundamental shift in consciousness. Experiential play therapy is a doorway where witnessing the "out picturing" of a child's inner world or what lives in his or her mind and heart unfolds, and although I would never encourage anyone to totally believe the words of a three-year-old, the goal of *We, the Children* is to have you believe the *play* of a three-year-old.

When adults unconsciously think of children as little adults and barrage them with questions as parents, guardians, interviewers, investigators, teachers, and so on, we actually prohibit or limit communication with them. Too much language blocks a child's truth. The best investigators and therapists know that toys are their tools when it comes to exchanging information with a little one. The question of children's rights in this book, which haunts me, is this:

Why should any child whom an adult has violated and can show this abuse through his or her play and behaviors have to endure being in the presence of his or her abuser *with no say in the matter,* because what children play doesn't count in court? Then, years later, when children are six or ten, sixteen or thirty-six, they find their voice and do what they've been taught to do; they tell a trusted adult.

Even after verbalizing the abuse, few adults believe these statements, and the perpetrator decrees that the child has been "coached." Yes, there are times when children *are* coached or told to say or feel something that actually belongs to someone else, the other parent, the grandparent, or whoever has an agenda of his or her own. The "casting of a spell" is often the metaphor used to illustrate coaching or programming. Almost always silence ensues regarding abuse after a perpetrator threatens to kill a child or her mother, father, family member, or pet if the truth be told.

Children can show this threat and few talk about it. So many children take on the role of family protector when they are in dire need of protection themselves. Such is the courage of the young child. Sometimes on rare occasions, even the youngest child's disclosure is believed. Usually the young adult or older child who discloses abuse is believed, or at least an investigation of some worth takes place. The child who can only play about his or her abuse is generally subject to more time spent with his or her abuser. And readers can imagine how this impacts the entire family negatively, rendering everyone as powerless as the child.

Powerlessness and a need for control go hand in hand however those feelings manifest. Certainly this new generation who already feel powerless over the world they are inheriting, appear to be either living with super-controlling behaviors or seem to be masters at going with the flow, caretaking and peace making. It's as if the extreme ends of their expression of love, rage, fear, frustration, confusion or feelings of apathy are an over-compensation for the imbalance of the world and the powerlessness they feel otherwise.

So when we do what we can where we live maybe we can be of assistance. Recognizing the wisdom and simple brilliance of child speak or child-created metaphors contributes to discovering the truth of a child's experience. These are first-world problems. But this is a first-world problem for children now living in the Western world, because in some ways, like in Syria, it's a most dangerous world for children, just on a different level. Sometimes, though it is more insidious and harder to detect, it is still somehow driven by our conscious and unconscious beliefs—not only about children but also about ourselves as humans. When we don't care about killing children in the streets, I doubt we will invest much in worrying about the truth of a child's domestic life situation. But murder is murder. And now here are their stories.

CHAPTER THREE

The Children's Stories

The Pile of None

A very anxious mother came in for therapy regarding her five-year-old girl, whom she had adopted from China at eight or nine months of age. Her mother reported that Jade's behavior was extremely defiant and aggressive toward her peers, showing high levels of anxiety and anger. And to top it off, she also had a problem with sleepwalking. According to her mother's intake information, Jade's teenage mother had abandoned her on the streets of a Chinese village as a newborn. An officer of the law later picked her up and delivered her to a nearby orphanage. Her mother assured me that Jade knew she was adopted (as an only child) but hadn't been told of her fragile origins. During this initial session Jade's mother outlined the known history of her daughter's life and the behaviors she was exhibiting.

Jade attended twenty-six experiential play therapy sessions in combination with her mother, her mother, her father, and alone (and to be clear, the therapist was witness to her journey). During her fifth session, Jade selected a tiny baby from one of the hundreds of miniatures and put it on the floor. Next she chose a police officer and placed him by the baby. She then took a treasure box designed to connote a person's worth and value; she scattered the treasure's contents, forcefully knocking over and burying the baby and the officer in a pile of glittering rubble. Satisfied with her play, Jade, with outstretched arms and tiny fingers spread open, declared to us, "See! The pile of none!"

This metaphor stands out as one of the most brilliant and succinct metaphors I've witnessed from a child. At five, Jade couldn't talk about her feelings, her sense of worthlessness and anger, feelings that were controlling her behavior and ability to progress developmentally, but she could certainly show them through her play. In one of her sessions, Jade also gave her mother the jaw-dropping experience of witnessing her replay her initial flight from China to the United States.

In her twenty-sixth and final session, Jade posed for a family photo with her parents and held a baby doll she had chosen and used as her self-object. Throughout therapy this baby doll helped Jade heal from the neglect and ridicule she'd experienced in the orphanage. It also allowed her to redo her infancy with her parents now.

This healing works primarily because the mind rewires itself according to experiences and emotions, allowing Jade to attach and bond with her adoptive parents at five because she'd missed the opportunity as an infant. In the square frame of my camera, Jade hugged her new self-object to her heart. A newborn baby doll, complete with an umbilical cord, embodied her need to bond with her adoptive parents from birth or before her birth. Sitting between her mother and father, having experienced true bonding and attachment on the developmental level of a newborn, she was free to grow up. Jade is smiling in this picture. Having joined with her adoptive family, she simultaneously joined with humanity. Play therapy allowed Jade to meet us at the developmental level where she was at – infancy – a stage she had to re-visit in order to heal and move on.

Successful interaction with small children is like balancing on a high wire, where one critical moment follows the next. Adults can learn to leap backward by becoming willing to leave the comfortable and neat world of intellectualism and cognition and take the difficult journey back into the messy world of sensations, symbols, and raw emotions that comprise the truth of childhood journeys.

The therapeutic playroom may be unique in providing little people a rare opportunity to unscramble eggs. In turn, this allows the child to change how he or she experiences himself or herself and his or her relationship to the world at large in a positive way.

A young child's play is a direct reflection of the child's inner and outer world; it is certainly the most accurate descriptor. Simply put, when children play, they talk or communicate; if you want to be close to children, play with them.

Tea with an Alien and a Werewolf

As you continue to move through the doorway into child speak and the inner world of children—how they process and what they see and understand at the deepest level of humanity—you may experience feelings of disbelief and of wanting to counter the subject of interpretation from the therapist.

What I know experientially and intuitively is that these stories contain both recognition and validation of what is true for the child rather than merely being an interpretation. In play therapy, particularly with very young children under the age of six or so, play is their language, and toys represent their words; toys, art, and music extend the child's vocabulary. Being able to play out their experiences and feelings allows children to communicate at their developmental level. Since 65 to 85 percent of all communication is nonverbal, it isn't so hard to see how this might work. About 99 percent of children who enter a therapeutic playroom have experienced intense emotions, trauma, or some kind of damage to their sense of dignity and worth. *Recognizing* and *witnessing* are better terms to describe the therapist's experience in the playroom than simple and suspect interpretation and the implication that what is played isn't necessarily true in its essence. In reality, everything is open to subjective interpretation or perception, but the chill or thrill of recognition is visceral, primal, and known throughout one's being to be true.

When an adult tells a story of trauma, I'm able to recognize trauma for what it is and need no interpretation at all. Trauma of any kind causes all humans to move into the right-brain system of emotions, collapsing the systems of logic until the bath of red-hot lava feelings cool off. Chances are, most of us will recognize traumatic experiences for what they are. Even hearing about someone's horrible experiences can shift the listener into his or her primitive right-brain system.

Sooner than later, we all experience the right-brain flush of an intense emotional flood, which literally washes away our ability to exercise logic and reason. How many times when angry have you wondered why you said what you said or did what you did? Young children *live* in a right-brained, experiential world that is full of primitive and raw emotion. Only our right brains can fully communicate nonverbally. As we have learned, children accomplish this communication by creating metaphors that illustrate their experiences and feelings. They also show brain-imprinted associations to people, places, events, and objects.

While living in Colorado and working weekly as an experiential play therapist every Tuesday at three thirty, I shared tea with an alien and a werewolf. Most of us have witnessed someone we know or love who was suddenly possessed by his or her evil doppelganger when under the influence of toxic substances. Some of us heal from this experience; some don't. One out of eight abused children goes on to abuse his or her children. An astonishing number of variables will dictate who becomes an abuser or the victim.

Did I really have tea with an alien and a werewolf? Metaphorically speaking, I did. I only had to be with Josh's metaphor for an hour a week; Josh had to live it. It's a metaphor most of us recognize.

Josh was a six-year-old boy who played out his experiences in his home this way. The situation was this: the alcoholic mother coupled with a "rage-aholic" father during ugly divorce proceedings in process. Josh's play amply illustrated how his mother morphed into an ugly alien when drinking; his father was someone who turned into a mean werewolf when in a rage. This experience became the norm for Josh's life, as he aptly showed in therapy.

Josh chose the kitchen to play in, because in general the kitchen represents nurturing issues on the symbolic level. After weeks of expressing his anger in other ways, Josh got down to the business of showing me what his nurturing and home life were like. His mother had absolutely zero control over herself or her two children. His father was addicted to getting angry, being right, and making Josh's mother wrong at any price, including his children's sense of well-being and safety.

In a therapeutic playroom, children are the directors and producers of the real-life movie they live in. To dramatize their experiences and process them, they often assign roles to the therapist or other participants in play therapy, much like the director does on a movie set. Josh assigned the role of being him to me while he played out the role of his mother preparing dinner while drinking alcohol. So I (as him) sat at the tiny table (waiting not only for dinner but also for some good nurturing) and witnessed the scene as he (as his mom) cooked and drank. Suddenly, he ran to the bin of puppets and masks, picked out the green rubber full-headed alien mask, complete with protruding purple, plastic almond-shaped eyes. He then turned his attention from the stove to me. Then Josh grabbed the werewolf mask, directing me to wear it, ordering me to growl as children do when experiencing a primal level of fear regarding their survival. Using a bop bag to represent himself (a large plastic egg-shaped figure) while sitting at the table, the alien and the werewolf shared a pot of pretend tea together, showing that this insane scene had become his normal nurturing experience. Josh had become a scapegoat, a punching bag for his parents' unhealed and angry wounds, unleashed not only on each other but also on their children. For many a Tuesday afternoon, we sat at the tiny table and pretended to drink tea as if there was nothing strange or frightening about it.

My blood chilled as the perfect metaphor of alien sank in; when drinking alcohol, his mom morphed into some terrifying, unknown creature, which had seemingly taken possession of her; for a child there is no other acceptable explanation. After all, this terrifying being "can't be my mother"! (The tendency to describe adults in a rage as a "monster" distorts many a child's testimony, causing the truth to be discarded as nonsense, when, in fact, it is a coping mechanism of children to do so.) Facing the reality of parental rage and fear causes children to shift their perceptions that a monster suddenly appears as a defense, plain and simple. After all, how do you survive if your caretakers are monsters? And then, who are you? A little monster?

Therapists are not immune to these events. Chills shot through my spine as the bright Colorado sun streamed through the playroom windows. I sat with this child's core fears, ignoring not only the proverbial elephant in the living room but also the alien and the werewolf at the kitchen table. I know that just having pretend tea validated his frightening journey, because I shared it with him and honored the difficulty of his life. This is the courage it takes to live life with crazy adults.

I'm pretty sure that Josh hadn't read *The Strange Case of Dr. Jekyll and Mr. Hyde,*[1] but his play illustrates that as children, we see the true and often hidden reality of life—the essence of what is. Mr. Stevenson believed that humans possessed two personalities. The character of Dr. Jekyll embodied the curious, married, healer – a well-regarded physician. Mr. Hyde represents the embodiment of our dark side – the murderer, the animal. Brilliant in its day, this story holds up to this day.

The adult world too often discounts, overlooks, or misunderstands the child's perspective of seeing with x-ray child eyes. This prejudicial and untutored attitude is especially unfair when it comes to allegations of abuse and decisions deciding parenting time and plans.

When adults assume that play themes aren't a legitimate means of communicating an experiential reality, we discount not only the children but also ourselves and our own childhood wounds. We are living in a time when healing from our wounded-ness is essential to our emotional survival. It's pretty easy for unaware parents, predators, and pedophiles to hide behind the idea that children's play is nonsense or invalid (akin to shooting fish in a barrel). Most significantly, children's voices and the truth they proclaim are silenced. Sadly and unjustly, their testimony is considered invalid, and perpetrators are free to roam to find their next victim. I try to remember - I try to believe that inside every bad guy, there is a good guy; it's just that sometimes that good guy is buried too deeply to be helpful to the child.

Serving Others

I could relate to this child's fears at the time, but as I considered Josh's story while writing it, I remembered the summer when I was two and a half years old and vacationing on Shelter Island. I split apart from my essential innocent self while witnessing my mother turn into Medusa with snakes crawling out of her eyes and head when she looked at me accusingly. This occurred when I innocently reported the events of a car ride I had with my father that morning after I jumped back into bed with her. My childhood was a perfect training ground for seeing what can occur behind closed doors, and it's precisely why I'm good at what I do.

Simply put, my father was my first lover, and my mother was my first enemy. Although, from the outside looking in, we appeared to be a typical family of the 1950s, terrible 1950's, terrible secrets lurked behind the white and closed doors. My perception of my mother as Medusa was just the beginning of a fractured and traumatic childhood. It led to a heavily checkered but amazingly healing and magical life, one in which I was blessed with work that gifted healing and understanding to children as well as to myself.

Way back in the 1950s, a time heralded as the best times to be a child, lurking behind the facade of sanity and security created by the end of World War II, and behind the arrival of Westinghouse, booze, the centrality church, family gatherings, and prosperity, the shadow side of my family oozed its evil vibrations and behaviors into my body, mind, and soul. In my unconscious mind, I absorbed the evil and duplicity I lived with. When I almost died in 2002 from a perforated appendix (who gets that?) I realized I caused my illness with my toxic thoughts of self-hatred. Self-loathing is the true result of child abuse. I now appreciate myself and even my mistakes and I still have my appendix.

These physical and emotional wounds took a lifetime to heal, but they did. Now, after having heard and witnessed terrifying childhood experiences over the past thirty-two years from thousands of people, I speak not only for the mistreated children but also for the countless, tireless therapists and child advocates out there who work in the inner domain with children and adults.

It is in this inner world of the child (and the inner child) that the secrets of truth reside and can be revealed; then true healing can happen.

My life is a miracle as I experience the healing that took almost sixty years to occur. After all, I work with children because I healed my very challenging passage to maturity; it is my dharma, and the children intuitively know that I get it and have lived it. Don't underestimate children or their ability to reveal what is their truth or their ability to wake up from even the worst nightmares (if they are believed, yes, and once again honored for their courage).

Divided by Divorce

One thing all children know is whether they receive good nurturing. This generation demands good nurturing. Divorce is one of the events in a child's life that severely disrupts nurturing. Although divorce, for example, has become almost as commonplace as marriage, there can be terrible effects on the child caught in the middle of a highly conflicted divorce. Children are the sacrificial lamb of this experience; there is no right or politically correct way to state this. Once upon a time, these parents were, at the least, attracted to each other; now the overriding need to be right or extract revenge makes a difficult situation a tragedy. The most common manifestation of this problem is that two good parents diligently fight for sole custody for years instead of using all that powerful energy to raise their child. All the intensely negative energy is used to win, to dismiss the other parent and all the stress, money, and conflict to be right. But this is just a waste and frankly a breach of a sacred contract with the littles.

When will adults learn that negative or positive statements family members say about other family members translate into labeling the same insults about the child to the child's sense of identity? It's really that simple. Let's practice the responsible use of words and acknowledge their power.

Typically, children of divorce divide things in half. Taking a sword and declaring that the bop bag is "split in two" is one of the many expressions of feeling torn or divided. Anyone who has had more than one home at a time and doesn't really like to pack or travel knows how stressful this can be, yet we expect young children to easily adapt to this arrangement when we couldn't do so ourselves. Parenting plans have children going to Dad's place for two days, then Mom's place for three days or a week on and a week off or Wednesday night with Dad or Thursday afternoons with Mom. These schedules can be crazy-making for everyone.

As every commissioner or judge knows, developing a parenting plan to last two years can take over two years. Since they are outside the child's experience, these vitally important decisions regarding one's childhood can only be lumped into large categories relating to age, stage of development and, to a lesser extent, the habits and lifestyle of the parents. It is clear to me that most children at least deserve a vote.

The child or children caught in the crossfire of parental war keep many secrets hidden during a hateful divorce. Often it's a he-said, she-said situation between adults, and children lose their voices entirely. Unless their therapist or Court Appointed Child Advocate worker or other advocate speaks up for them.

Children are quite adept at playing that scene of a war no one ever wins to illustrate and process the conflict. Everyone loses in divorce, according to the child. All those involved display their distress and transitional issues, going from one home to the other (often remarkably enough) by using bridges that take them from castles to houses. They frantically run back and forth until I get it and verbally validate this chaotic experience. Admittedly, divorce, the creation of parenting plans, and so on are more than complicated issues. The point is, children deserve a vote.

Children learn first and foremost from adult actions and words, because these reflect true beliefs, attitudes, and values. "I don't have time" could be the slogan of our advances in technology. Oh sure, sometimes texting saves time, but we all know the day could come when a supernova knocks it all out, and then what? Anxiety is the diagnosis of the millennium.

I've known hundreds of divorcing parents, so here are some divorce stories from the child's perspective. It's not that I'm judging the act of divorce. I'm referring to the unconscious assumptions about the actual effect of a divorce on each and every individual child—your child—and how learning about these effects can ease the pain of separation.

Josh's story emerged from a highly conflicted divorce, but agreeable divorces create their own powerful emotions and stories, as you'll read in Zack's story:

Zack was three when his parents divorced. By four, he was a mess. He cried constantly, wet his bed, whined all the time, and refused to use a bathroom away from one of his homes. As a person, Zack combined the gifts of a poet and a scientist, and he used the playroom as his laboratory. He had good parents. Zach's parents were always polite to each other and seemingly kind on the surface—which is, of course, better than screaming, hating, or being picky. But the repressed anger and resentment generated by an affair and the subsequent abandonment of divorce echoed an invisible but palpable energy for Zack to deal with.

In his first play therapy session, after he cut the bop bag in half (repeating a common practice for children of divorce), he built a volcano in the sand. Volcanoes were important to Zack to symbolize anger and how he tried to manage it by crying nonstop or whining. Zack stood before the sand table, which touched his waist. His little hands caressed the sand, letting it cascade and slip through his fingers. The sands of time and missed opportunities escaped through his fingers. He whispered, "Sometimes the sand is like the pure-driven snow ..."

He used wet, oozy, squishy Play-Doh to illustrate the creepy, icky feelings he had inside. "That is sooo yukky!" we would commiserate, our eyes locking together through shared perception. One day Zack was shooting marbles. He pointed to the shooter and the marble he'd shot, and he observed, "Do you know what makes that marble move right there?"

"No, what?" (I almost always play dumb with children.)

"It's momentum," he proudly announced.

"Yes, Zack, you are so right" I agreed. Then the proverbial light went on in my mind. I was able to make the communication leap: "I guess even invisible things have a lot of power."

He smiled broadly. We were communicating deeply about the emotional charge that still stung Zach every time he was in the presence of both of his parents. The relief we both felt by decoding his metaphor was profound. The tensions his parents were trying so hard to hide from Zack were actually impeding his development. His parents had to learn that what they believed to be in the best interest of their child wasn't. What comprises the best interest of the child is generally best learned *from the child.*

Further review of the research shows that children practice for life (similar to a dress rehearsal) and achieve higher levels of brain functioning through play. Schools that have used the Tools Programs[1] or other play-based education have shown a significant increase in functionality and assimilation of information—in short, executive functioning, including a decrease in aggression and apathy—to the point that these schools lost their funding due to not being in dire straits anymore. Go figure. (There are those who oppose thought systems again.)

But what we learned from the Tools Program is that if you ask children to stand still for as long as they can, they last about one minute or less. When they are asked to *pretend* to be soldiers standing at attention, they stand still for eleven minutes. Thus, they teach self-regulation, self-confidence, and a feeling of organization and social grace just by playing fire station (or something like that) in scripted roles for forty-five minutes a day. And they therefore learn self-control through play.

Role-playing in schools illustrated that children's cognition develops more quickly and better when playing than by getting direct instruction. This is just one of the examples in the book *NutureShock* by Po Bronson and Ashley Merrryman.

In experiential play therapy, children often plan their sessions after the first time or two in the playroom. When urgent unconscious or conscious memories prompt them, they play them out. They can't help it. When this is done effectively, the responses of the therapist move the play forward, so to speak, positively affecting cognition, social behavior, and emotional regulation indirectly and with more efficiency. Play is to children what wings and air are to birds and toys can serve as their words.

Toys are selected for their projective value. In other words, toys with pre-assigned roles or personalities (such as Batman or Elsa from *Frozen*) are not considered particularly therapeutic. Neutral toys encourage and allow expression by projection of emotional experiences and developmental challenges. A child develops life themes in the playroom according to his or her ability to do so and dramatizes events that are stressful, confusing, or otherwise challenging to the child who can't move on fully until this event or experience is mastered. Playing with a trained therapist, whose responses are constructed not only to support the child in his or her heroic journey, to validate their courage, but to move the play toward the resolution of the problems to the child's developmental ability. Obviously, supportive home environments increase the pace and success of this process.

Without going religious, let me say that this truth was understood over two thousand years ago . "When I was I child, I talked like a child, thought like a child, I reasoned as a child. When I became a man, I put childish ways behind me".[2]

As an experiential play therapist, I've had to resist pressure from parents and other adults to use traditional adult-type therapies with children and talk them out. Children express feelings and experiences in words but generally not before age five or six; then they will do so in brief, concise, and often mysterious sentences. In fact, these days there is more and more pressure to use talk therapy with young children until the parent gets it.

Experiential play therapy is based on theories of development from Erickson's stages of development to current theorists on play therapy. Although children may develop faster now, the fundamental stages of development still need to occur successfully to produce a healthy adult. Because, according to Erickson's theory of development, children are either developing hope, will, a sense of purpose, competency, fidelity and love or their growth is stunted by lack of committed nurturance. Demanding that children verbalize or talk about their experiences forces them to operate in a way they are too immature to engage in and can result in missed opportunities for experiential play that can grow a healthier brain; the talking comes later.

Children perceive language as a form of adult control. To talk about their experiences, children have to force their thoughts through a sieve of language, which is narrow at best, and fit their sensory world into a box consisting of words, much like having to speak in a foreign language when you know only a few rudimentary words or phrases of that language. Play and pretend or fantasy allows children to process their world their way; it is *pre*operational, like children.

It's up to the adult to find meaning in a child's play that is congruent with the child who, believe me, will let you know whether you are seeing it wrong. Fantasy or pretend play not only allows children to learn new sets of rules about life, self-regulation, and relationships but also allow children to create their worlds without the constraints of making their metaphoric creations understandable to the adult, although they certainly are capable of doing so. In short, play is essential to childhood development and is necessary for growth to occur.

I have seen children who left therapy in an incomplete state of processing return six months later and, in spite of six more months of living, pick up exactly where they left off in the playroom—like picking up an interrupted conversation.

As you will read in later sections of *We, the Children*, kids can come to therapy at age five, but because they experienced trauma or loss at age two, they will work on their trauma or loss from that developmental stage. They may indeed temporarily regress to that part of their life, both in the playroom and outside in the world. (There's that development thing again; how many two-year-old forty-year-olds do *you* know?) It is so powerful. I generally remind parents that to have a five-year-old regress to two is much better than trying to confront and change a teenager who never had the opportunity to "fix" incomplete, inadequately completed, or downright traumatized or missed stages of development. When you see an adult "acting like a child," this is why. Humans can pretend to be at a higher level of development than they are experiencing in reality, but this facade always breaks down sooner or later; humans simply have to move through each developmental stage successfully to grow and be healthy.

The play therapist provides a child with a sense of security and understanding through a relationship of unconditional acceptance of the child where he or she is. Good old Carl Roger's pioneer counseling theory, based on "unconditional positive regard," is embraced while the child recreates emotionally stressful experiences and works toward mastery. Oddly, many of the basic theories of human development are in action and "covered" in play therapy. Although hidden within the context of play, cognition is improved much in the same way that cognitive behavioral therapy (CBT) works with teens and adults to identify and challenge self-sabotaging beliefs and behaviors about oneself and one's abilities, and then to change those self-defeating thoughts into competency. Responses and feedback from the therapist also tucked away into play themes and often directed through the toys to preserve a child's dignity and identity, fit right into the CBT model but in a discreet or indirect manner.

Attachment theory is also related to play therapy in the sense that as children select toys and create metaphors in the playroom, in art, and in the sandbox to reflect their struggles and victories in life, the relationship with the therapist contributes to a sense of connectivity and of being heard, respected, and valued for just being who they are. When parents play with their children in the playroom or therapeutically at home, bonding and attachment can be healed, enhanced, and even achieved for the first time by engaging in therapeutic play.

Newer theories regarding the combined effect of genetics, nature, and nurture are also addressed experientially in the playroom. Children bring all the variables that make them who they are into the session, including temperament, family dynamics, socioeconomic status, genetic gifts and challenges, and how nurture interfaces with nature. It all happens in one fell swoop. This is an amazing statement to make and even outrageous to claim, but it's true in my experience. Play therapy helps children repair attachment breaks due to divorce.

> From the Children's Bill of Rights for Children of Divorce

Special Concerns of Children Committee, March 1998
When Parents Are Not Together

> Every kid has rights, particularly when Mom and Dad are splitting up. Below are some things parents shouldn't forget—and kids shouldn't let them—when the family is in the midst of a breakup.

You have the right to love both your parents. You also have the right to be loved by both of them. That means you shouldn't feel guilty about wanting to see your dad or mom at any time. It's important for you to have both parents in your life, particularly during difficult times, like the breakup of your parents.

You have the right to be in a safe environment. This means that nobody is allowed to put you in danger, either physically or emotionally. If one of your parents is hurting you, tell someone—either your parent or a trusted adult like a teacher.

You don't belong in the middle of your parents' breakup. Sometimes your parents may get so caught up in their own problems that they forget that you're just a kid and that you can't handle their adult worries. If they start putting you in the middle of their dispute, remind them that it's their fight, not yours.

Grandparents, aunts, uncles, and cousins are still part of your life. Even if you're living with one parent, you can still see relatives on your other parent's side. You'll always be a part of their lives, even if your parents aren't together anymore.

You have the right to be a child. Kids shouldn't worry about adult problems. Concentrate on your schoolwork, your friends, activities, and so forth. Your mom and dad [or dads and moms, author's addition] just need your love. They can handle the rest. *It's not your fault, and don't blame yourself.*[3]

The following are play therapy stories:

What Babies Remember

Taylor was two-years-old when her adoptive parents brought her to therapy. Taylor was eighteen months old when she was adopted. Her father was a preacher, and her mother a stay-at-home mom. In spite of their lack of funding, this couple adopted several at-risk children. Taylor, born of drug-addicted parents, had lived in a cocaine house for the first year and a half of her life, and now she came to therapy as a mere toddler. This toddler was developmentally tasked to re-do her infancy to gain trust and hope and safety for her life because her birth home had robbed her of that sense of worth and trust in life itself.

I was admittedly nervous at the thought of an angry toddler crashing through the playroom and wondered, *If so, how therapeutic would* that *be?*

A child that young can benefit from the playroom experience only when he or she is able to play with the toys symbolically, and most little ones can by two and a half but not all. This child, however, was a whole other story and a remarkable illustration of how accurately even a child of trauma can not only remember her experiences but also play them out.

During Taylor's initial visit, she surveyed the playroom with big brown eyes from a standing-still posture close to her mother's side. She checked out the room of toys without moving anything but those eyes, as she worked on how to organize her story and make sure she was safe in doing so. She communicated right away that her stillness was a survival behavior she had learned to assess the mood of the adults who were supposed to be taking care of her. She wanted to assess whether it was safe to be hungry, wet, or cold—or to have any infant needs at all.

By about her third or fourth session, Taylor selected a king figure, who clearly became the "snowman," representing the drug dealer or head honcho in the money and control department of the drug world she lived in. This king figure held the most power, indicated by a lightning rod in his hand; he also wore a crown and cape, strutting his power as the dealer for all to see. Then she chose the smallest of baby dolls available to her in the playroom and threw it into the corner of the room, leaving it to lie neglected and abandoned. She showed that in her birth home, she wasn't considered important or valuable. Saddest of all, she felt discarded, rejected, unwanted, and unloved.

I was amazed by her ability to play at such a deep level, a level she could never have expressed if she had to rely on words or, simply put, to speak as an adult. No one can speak adult at two, no matter how smart he or she is.

Taylor continued to use the Play mobile toys to show people of various races, ages, and gender going in and out of the house. People fell down and were out of control and unstable. Some slumped in their chairs as the king stomped around, wielding his lightning rod of power (he was the man; he had the drugs; he was the pusher, he had control and power). From a dirty and forgotten corner of the room, this tiny baby witnessed the whole scene in mute silence to survive in a very hostile and invalidating environment. *Invalidating* is putting it mildly, and yet this child was fully capable of showing her experience during infancy in the playroom in only a few short hours of therapy. Taylor verbalized in a session with her mother, "The daddy and mommy see it." Her little fingers pointed to the baby in the corner (her self-object). "She [the baby] knew what was going on, and she didn't break apart."

Taylor demonstrated an off-the-charts resiliency and completed therapy after about twenty sessions as a happy and compassionate little girl. She had become part of an extended family that included other siblings adopted out of painful, uncaring, invalidating, and unconscious families of origin.

And then there was Adam, who was three years old when his mother became very concerned about his behavior. He had started crawling around on all fours and growling at his peers and certain family members. Adam was extremely bright and sensitive in nature. He had become unable to play with friends or attend preschool, because his fear of people increased to an intolerable level, and his attempts to frighten everyone away were working. How could Adam enjoy or even try to experience normal development while almost constantly pretending to be a fearsome animal (to keep his own fears in check)? Clearly, he couldn't.

Adam was what I call a classic case of play therapy, as he progressed through the five stages of treatment textbook style in twelve sessions. Adam was a verbal child who actually explained his metaphors as he played. (They should all be so easy to understand.) He told his story as he used the toys to reenact his experiences.

Adam chose pigs to represent his family, with a mother and papa pig who had one baby. In one session, while playing in the sand, Adam showed the parent pigs, and in particular the mother pig, searching for her lost piglet. The baby pig was trapped in a smoke-filled container (his words) and desperately longed for his mother. It was an intuitive leap to later ask his mother whether he'd had a difficult birth or an early and traumatic separation from her. (This led to the development of an extensive medical history in my practice, but Adam was one of my first clients.)

I'll never forget the look of shock on his mother's face; her eyes widened, and she gasped. "How could you possibly know that? He was in an incubator for five days, right after he was born, and I wasn't allowed to hold him or anything; it was a very sad time." Three-year-old Adam not only reenacted his development-stopping birth experience in a systemic way, but as we were preparing to say good-bye, he'd check in with me, saying, "Don't be sad that I'm leaving. It's okay." When he left therapy, Adam was able to attend preschool successfully and no longer needed to growl or be a scary animal to cope with his fears and the world.

Children feel emotions deeply and personally. Most children have an innate sense of fairness and need help to understand an unfair world or situation. Seemingly, an inner life force governs most children and propels them into a positive sense of self and a desire to grow and be healthy and successful. Simply put, most children intuitively know exactly how to heal themselves in this process and take the therapeutic experience where they need it to go to grow. Children certainly know what good nurturing is, and they know when they aren't getting that. This new generation won't tolerate sloppy nurturing; in fact, parents, teachers, police, and others all have to work 200 percent to raise, teach, or uncover the truth of the child today. As trusting as most children are, they are wary and perceptive when it comes to relating to adults.

Naturally, some children are more resilient than others, and this resiliency is easily witnessed in their lives and their ability not only to express concerns and challenges through play but also to correct or heal them. I have witnessed over two thousand children overcome tremendous odds, partly assisted by the play therapy process. I have seen children overcome abuse of all kinds, including multiple losses and traumas. They just have to sort out being human, feeling overloaded with information and sensory data and be granted the time to do so.

We are mysterious beings, and this fact is most evident in childhood. Contrary to some popular beliefs about children, truth, and our current systems for improving or directing the life of children, most children don't lie, and when they do, telling when they are is hard. (Except when only you and the child are present and the cookie or cupcake is not and you know you didn't eat it.) The older a child becomes, the more likely he or she will tell stories to please an adult, to trick an adult, to just experiment with words, or even to see what they can get away with, what happens when they don't tell the truth, or of course in order to avoid trouble. The body is a communication device, and children know this fact inherently and unconsciously. It is almost 100 percent impossible for the body to lie, (this could be why so texting is more comfortable than face-to-face encounters or even voice encounters) especially in younger children. Play therapy is most reliable in terms of the child's experience simply because it isn't simply a cognitive process in the sense of using words to describe experiences or feelings; it is experiential and brain-changing.

Experiential play is virtually impossible to coach or direct through adult direction. It is especially impossible to write or teach a script that I child could sustain consistently throughout an entire session or series of sessions over time. So when children play and talk about feeling abused, misused, or hurt, they know what they are playing and talking about. In court, most child play is disregarded due to the trouble with interpretation versus recognition; however, many adults, trained or untrained, would *recognize* unhealthy, maladaptive play, especially if it was their own child playing it.

What Babies Remember (Continued)

Six-year-old Jessie came in for therapy due to displaying extremely aggressive behaviors at home and especially at school toward her peers. She often scratched or poked other children. Jessie was in first grade and displayed a sneering disregard and disrespect toward adults in general and certainly toward her teacher. This was a double paradox because Jessie presented herself in Laura Ingalls style, complete with her hair drawn back with ribbons and long *Little House on the Prairie*-style dresses. Her parents were a committed, fun-loving couple, and their son was only a few years younger than Jessie. They wanted to give Jessie all the advantages in life, but something was clearly wrong. This story is like the others.

When I met Jessie, I encountered the mask she presented to the world. Her hair was tied halfway up, princess style, with the modest dress and little black dress shoes; she was meek in appearance. Jessie was described as often angry, especially at her toddler brother. She was a compassionate and polite, intelligent child, but she now described herself as "stupid."

In the eighties, there was a huge wave of child abuse being recognized and reported, sometimes with false accusations. There was a focus on abuse in the day care setting. The following excerpt is taken from Jessie's intake session with just her mother.

> The day care woman called me at work one day to say that Jessie had hit her forehead. It was swollen and about the size of an egg—the woman said she fell out of her walker and hit her head on the dog's food bowl. Jessie was about nine months old when this occurred. Looking back on this incident, I can't really say that I believed her. Soon after that, we took Jessica to a regular preschool, and then, when that didn't work out, a third one. Jessie was asked to leave the preschools due to aggressive behaviors. When she was about three and a half, we found a wonderful in-home day care woman (at last) to take care of her, and she stayed there until she started school that fall.
>
> Jessie's play, it turned out, referred back to when she was nine months old. Her mind and spirit were bent in the wrong direction because of things she'd witnessed and endured as an infant.

It was revealed through investigating into this case more deeply that the woman who told Jessie's mother about her falling out of a walker, which we all know is pretty darn difficult, was reported to social services for being unlicensed, even after she'd assured parents that she was a licensed day care provider. It's not that a license decides the quality of the care, but a person willing to take the steps to be licensed may also be inclined to take better steps in caring for children.

Once Jessie established trust in me and in the process, she showed me that when she was less than one year of age, she'd witnessed the woman (who was reported) breaking another child's arm. In fact, Jessie's mother remembered the incident when the little boy was rushed to the emergency room. But again, the day care provider had stated the injury was due to an accident.

Jessie's reputation for being a bully, incongruous as this appeared, stemmed from her attempt to keep others safe by scaring them away from her. As a baby who witnessed the abuse of other children, the imprint in Jessie's brain told her that she was dangerous. A red streak of fear and the adrenaline of terror rerouted a healthy baby brain into one of terror and misunderstandings. Jessie believed that others were hurt due to her presence. Because all children and certainly infants are naturally egocentric, they just experience that all that happens because of them. At nine months there were no clear dividing lines between Jessie and "others." Her sense of self was undefined at best. In other words, she didn't know that she didn't hurt the other children; the lines of self

> were blurred. It has been said that the abused takes on the energy of the abuser, often believing themselves to be evil (as in the case of Sarah told later). Jessie internalized that other children were in danger if they were near her, and in her attempt to protect them she was mistaken as a bully because that is how her behavior appeared. This is how children learn what we are not trying to teach them and how convoluted our assumptions can become.

If she had been punished for this behavior, Jessie might never have healed from her mistaken impressions of herself, and no one knows what her life might have been like without intervention. I've met plenty of Jessies in the juvenile justice system as teenagers who never stood a chance.

In one significant session, Jessie created a wet mountain of sand in the sand table and worked hard on making tunnels in the wet, dark sand. She instructed me to meet her "down under." Laughing with utter relief as our fingers "found" each other in the dark, cold place, which allowed us to hold hands inside her tunnel, I said to her, "Our fingers and hands are meeting in a cold, dark place. It's okay now because no one is alone there anymore." Jessie's healing process sped up after having the experience of not being alone in the cold, dark imprinting of violence into her infant brain. She started to rewire her experience of herself because it felt like there was a safe adult trusting her goodness *back then*.

This story illustrates the power of play; this is how children communicate, process and heal.

Here is one more fascinating story involving the granddaughter of a pastor of a huge church in Colorado. She was also six years old when she came to therapy. Her presenting issues read like this: "Fear of school, anxiety regarding bullying at school, concern regarding the school's response to Kali's problems, sudden shift in behavior with no prior problems with Kali."

Over the course of her therapy, Kali reenacted her experience with trauma on the playground. Recess, I've learned, can be deadly. Apparently, an older boy both verbally threatened Kali while she was playing and violently kicked her for no apparent reason. *She* was disciplined and told to "go stand by the wall." Kali was so frightened and angry.

Kali told me through her play and her words that the older boy had controlled her by telling her that he would kill her baby sister, her, and her family by "taking a chair and smashing her head in and watching her bleed." As I write this, I hesitate to think where that boy is today; he encouraged other boys to jump on her back and kick her in the back and privates. Her accusations of abuse by the boys was supported by her play themes, the school psychologist, as well as her verbal and nonverbal reenactments of terror.

Because the human mind strings associated events together, Kali kept playing about, being a "crawling baby" who was terrified of dying. Additionally, she played being at preschool age and wrestling with a dark figure in her bedroom. I told her grandfather, who usually brought her to therapy, that something traumatic had happened to Kali during the first year of her life. He took offence and stated emphatically that she hadn't experienced any trauma in her first year or in preschool.

Because she kept playing this situation, I kept insisting that it was so until one day the light bulb in her mother's brain lit up. She said, "Oh! I remember now what it was! We were in the shower; I was holding her over my shoulder and showering with her. She was about eight or nine months old. Water went down her throat, and she started to choke. It felt like a long time until she could catch her breath. For a minute we were afraid she would pass out, become unconscious, or stop breathing! For a moment, we thought she might die."

Stringing her traumatic experiences together formulated the basis for Kali's terror when she believed she would die. After that, the grandfather sent me a lot of clients.

In twelve short sessions, Kali worked through her fears. Her mother shared one other story from Kali's preschool age: "When she was three, we got her a bed in her room. But my stepmother was an alcoholic and lived and died in that room. Several times, we witnessed and were terrified by a black shape that floated over Kali's bed. We arranged a house blessing. We think it was Grandma Trudy trying to feed off her innocent energy." Wow. We never know what a family or a little child is experiencing.

> There is a way
> Between voice
> And presence
> Where information
> Flows.
> In disciplined
> Silence it opens.
> With wandering
> Talk it closes.
> Rumi[4]

CHAPTER FOUR

Child Sexual Abuse

Back in the early 1990s, one of the stories that peaked my interest in experiential play therapy was told by Dr. Byron Norton, PhD, originator of experiential play therapy.

Parents went to Byron because they suspected child abuse from the day care their daughter was attending. At about three years old, this child was interviewed by the police and social workers. She was asked to describe where she had been when the bad thing happened. She said, "I could hear the bicycles and the birdies singing." Her story was both laughed at and disregarded, as the investigators believed the child was incapable of telling a truthful or coherent story. Later, after further investigation, other children emerged with similar stories, and investigators discovered that the room in which the abuse had taken place housed low windows that opened to a tree-lined and bird-filled bicycle path.

That little child had answered the question, but no one but Byron had spoken her language. Her therapist, with impressive credentials and years of experience, was found banging his proverbial head against the wall in the attempt to prove what had taken place during naptime. Afterward, when all the puzzle pieces were put together, some law enforcement agents and attorneys could see the validity and honesty of the child's answer. My best guess is that these professionals had children of their own.

Here is an excerpt from a child in therapy years ago. She was Chinese and spent her first year and a half in a Chinese orphanage, enduring sexual abuse and other abuse. Then she was adopted into the USA. Her parents, mature and wise adults, helped this child (I have renamed her Ginny) to heal her intense issues in seventeen sessions. This case was quite amazing.

This conversation illustrates the perfecting of the internalization of self-hatred that the abuse and neglect during her first year and a half produced in her brain and self-image. She healed rapidly, partly because of who she was and because her parents joined in her personal story so fully.

> I started to mention how many students were absent from her class today after talking with the school counselor. "What is this all about?" she asked. I asked whether she knew why her friend (Alyssa) hadn't been in school for two days, and she said, "Because of what happened in the bathroom?" Her confusion was evident. I told her that Alyssa's grandmother had talked to me today and told me it, (the sexualized bullying) happened again. Alyssa told her grandmother that "you squeezed her privates and told her not to tell or she'd get spanked." Ginny asked when it had happened. I told her Thursday after lunch. She was lying!
>
> For the next twenty to thirty minutes, Ginny felt hysterical and repeated, "I wish I was a pile of dirt! I wish I were dead! People say they care about me. Yeah, right. Why did you bring me

> here? To ruin my life! This is the end of my world; I hate my life. Why did you get me so upset? I think I'm most mad at you; I feel so mad that I could rip someone's face." I told her it was clear how upsetting all of this was and that it was a normal feeling for her to have. "Then why did you tell me? You just want to ruin my life." I told her I had to talk to her because Alyssa was too scared now to go to school and that the truth had to come out. I said it was hurting both of them a lot. "More!" she shouted. "It's hurting me more! I have a worse feeling than her! I told her I knew she could get through this … etc."
>
> Ginny repeated over and over that she would never go back to school, never look at Alyssa again … that Alyssa was lying … She said, "Am I sinning and I don't even know it? I couldn't do it again? I promised my mother I'd never do it again. I feel like a crime … I am a criminal! I don't believe you care; my parents don't even care about me."[1]

The critical issue here is that child abuse of any kind imposes a life sentence on the receiver, even when the healing occurs. A person is not ever completely like it never happened. Children are unique in their responses to sexual abuse. Some withdraw, some act out, some are angry or terrified, keeping secrets; one thing is certain—the child's behavior and play will change, and anyone paying attention will get the creeps. Approximately one out of eight children who are sexually abused goes on to abuse others.[2]

When I worked with addictions and adults, which I did for eleven years, I met a thirty-six-year-old woman who had been her father's sexual partner all her life. She needed help grieving the loss of that relationship through his death, and she never even recognized the debilitating and distorted nature of her entire life in relation to her father.

Currently, because of the incredible intelligence of the youngest of our generations, their ability to communicate with words, art, play, or always behaviors—secret or revealed—is even more accurate than ever. However, very young children may still seek to protect the perpetrator, themselves, their pets, or their other parent, whose abuser might have threatened their very lives in different ways.

Attorneys, judges, interviewers, and visitation supervisors need to spend more time truly listening to children's testimonies by *actually considering these disclosures as testimonies or possible evidence.* Then the professionals on a case need to err on the side of caution to protect the child, or else they are guilty of the same abuse that has been perpetrated on the child. Furthermore, teaching children that they are powerless to speak and be heard, that telling does no good at all, and that the people they did trust are rendered as powerless as they are is truly missing the mark.

Just recently, I was playing with a child, about eight years old, who showed a queen and princess hiding from bad guys in a castle. This hiding was coupled with a clear need for protection. I didn't know until I received an email from her mother that when she was two, she and her mother had indeed hidden in a hotel from her father, who had just been served with a protection order from the court. I wasn't told about this event from her past until the mother recognized her play from her own daughter's history.

In *Return to Life*, Dr. Jim B. Tucker, MD, meticulously documented and seemingly verifies past life memories of very young children. If children can remember events from past lives why not remember early or implicit memories from this life?[3]

We know that the brain records every single event, word, experience, sight, sound, and smell as they happen. We also now know that the tenor and essence of those experiences construct the neural pathways in the developing brain, whether children experience trauma or good nurturing predicts many future options for each child. It simply communicates to a baby whether the world is safe or dangerous, whether the baby is valued.

These days even children who feel the safest perceive the world as dangerous, because it is. Child advocates and therapists who have had the experience of getting past the adult requirement to make children speak about their experiences know that children can and will reenact these experiences accurately and willingly according to their perceptions and developmental ability to do so. It is time that this ability to communicate is revisited and validated as a valid testimony to their life situations.

Child sexual abuse is not only difficult to see, but to this day, it is hard to believe and even harder to prove in court. Judges would do best to decide on the side of caution if a reasonable doubt is clearly presented through a child's verbal and nonverbal testimony, regardless of what the adults in the case have to say about it.

Even medical or physical evidence can be turned against innocent parents instead of child protectors who are seeking the true perpetrator, and often it is. I worked with a family of three children, who were sexually abused in a day care in Colorado. They had moved there from dangerous Miami, Florida, to find a safer place to raise their children. The youngest child was a girl of two and a half years old.

One night she fell asleep on the way home from day care. Her mother woke her up to feed her and give her a bath, only to her shock and horror to find blood in her diaper. The parents, who were good parents, immediately called CPS (child protective services), who almost immediately accused the father of sexually abusing his daughter and two sons. I worked with these children for countless hours for over a year, and because of the refusal or reluctance of the police and the CPS workers to listen to their stories, the perpetrators (at a father-and-daughter-run day care) were able not only to hide the evidence (because the police called to let them know they were coming) but also to leave the state freely to continue on somewhere else as a team of child sexual perpetrators, father and daughter style. Instead, the parents had to fight to prove their innocence.

After working with literally thousands of children, I have reported child sexual abuse no more than about ten times. With only one exception, I had to fight tooth and nail for the child to prove that this terrible event had occurred. Because of my history, I'm extremely cautious about reporting these allegations and suspicions of abuse. The law mandates that therapists report to the authorities even a suspicion of child abuse. Since most reports involving play testimony are disregarded, I wonder, *Who does the law or CPS think is perpetrating these crimes? As we now know, even the most trusted priests of religious orders, teachers, camp counselors, and coaches can be pedophiles or opportunistic perpetrators.* Child abuse is nothing new; we have justified hurting children and, therefore, ourselves from the Old Testament and beyond. Is this just the way we're built? Or can we return to our original selves—to the essential goodness within us all?

CHAPTER FIVE

See, Hear, and Speak No Evil

The following soul story involves a case of suspected sexual child abuse from the father. When I met Sarah while living in Colorado, she was too young to speak about things; she was only three and a half years old. When she turned five, the judge and everyone else said she had to talk, so she did after I told Sarah that the judge said she thought Sarah was a big girl who could talk about what happened, so that's what she needed to do. When she talked, they still didn't believe her. Typically, the response from the defense is that the other parent coached the child to lie. Coaching does happen sometimes. What doesn't happen is when a child plays about the same issues consistently for over a year; children cannot be coached about what to spontaneously play, and everyone knows it. No one can tell a child what to play for a year or more. The process is far too spontaneous of to be programmed; however, the child may show *being* programmed ("She cast a spell on me," for example), or a child may freeze in place (flight, fight, or freeze), but that's about as far as controlling a young child's play will go. And if children don't want to play, which is rare, but it happens upon occasion, nothing can make them.

Sarah talked with me one day, and this is what she said:

> "I told Mommy that Daddy hurt my body when he had a big spoon with a long handle, and he kept hitting me with it, and when he hit me, he said, 'Die, die.'"
>
> I said to Sarah, "I don't think your dad would say that to you, so you must remember not to say anything that isn't true."
>
> Sarah's response: "It is true. Daddy yelled at me, 'Die, die, die,' and he was very angry, and he hurt my feelings, and he hurt my back."
>
> I asked her: "Why was Daddy so angry with you?"
>
> Sarah responded: "I don't know, and I don't understand why he would always get so angry. One time I asked him if I could have some dinner, and he got so mad, he hit me on my back over and over."
>
> I asked: "Are you saying that this happened more than once?"
>
> Sarah said: "Yes, more than one. Daddy banged my back over and over, and I cried, but Daddy didn't listen to me. Daddy told me it was okay to jump on his bed. I was jumping and jumping. Then Daddy came into the room with no clothes on. I told him, 'Daddy, get your clothes on. You look stupid.' Daddy told me to take my clothes off. I told him I didn't want to, but he took my clothes off anyway. Daddy hurt my feelings, and he broke my heart. Every time Daddy took me back to Mommy's house in (her town), then Mommy put lots and lots of tape on my heart."

I repeat this story because this is the crux of my point in advocating for children. When Sarah came to therapy, she was three and a half years old and incapable of saying these words to anyone. And when she could, after disclosing her abuse to qualified therapists and attending more than two years of therapy, the very person hired to protect her, the guardian *ad litem*, a.k.a. the child's attorney or her assumed representative in court, disregarded her statements, her play, her therapists, mother and grandmother.

I don't know how much Sarah will remember or how she will feel as time goes on and she matures. Even after the trial, she had to spend "alone time" with her father, and she continued to report his molesting her and continued being ignored. Her mother was accused of coaching her; her therapists deemed incompetent. I do know that she has split into two parts: her "good" self and her "bad" self. She told me that when she is forced to drink the poison, (be sexual) she turns into her bad self or the black Pegasus—her story, her way. The black Pegasus and the While Pegasus fought in the air for dominance. Too bad everyone in power doesn't know it's not just fantasy, the battle between good and evil within us. In this story, where it had to leave off the bad guy won, every professional on the job was dismissed from the case. I hate to pit "us against them" but the "them" are those who do harm to another.

You know how we just don't remember everything from childhood. Our minds would be more insane than they are now. I have literally had the experience of watching as experiences, feelings, and events move from the conscious mind to the subconscious and are stored wherever we store our forgotten memories. I also have watched as new personalities tried to form. In this case, a child whose basic orientation to the world, her parents, and herself had become twisted into a bizarre perception because confronting the father was too frightening.

Her family and I waited and worked with Sarah, patiently giving her the time she needed to verbalize what she was fully capable of playing about for over two years. That is the point. Children's play will point to the truth if we can only decipher it. And this was another case that felt like I was going to court with the devil.

The father, the father's attorney, and the so-called guardian felt like natural predators doing their best job to discredit everyone but their unholy trio. In fact, the father was such an adept manipulator that I liked him for a while, even when I knew what he had done to his daughter! That feeling passed but not before he influenced everyone else who became involved in this case as transporter, supervisor, or attorney to see him favorably. I'm somewhat comforted by the fact that Ann Rule, grandmother of true crime, worked side by side with serial killer Ted Bundy at a suicide crises line and then stayed his friend and supported him throughout much of the trial. It was so hard to believe he could be the person the law showed to be. It's equally hard to believe that a nice person you know may be a child molester.

Would perpetrators draw attention to themselves? There would be a lot less child abuse if perpetrators were easy to spot, but the most adept predators are hard to pick out of a crowd and may never arouse suspicions. A sociopath who believes his own lies can pass a polygraph, so is passing a lie detector test all it's cracked up to be? Especially when you ask someone who lacks a conscience to tell the truth?

Believe me, that a guilty person can lie without blinking an eye or blipping a machine. According to the most recent inquiries into polygraphs, research has revealed that false positives are a real problem. There are folks who job it is to teach people how to pass those tests. National Public Radio (NPR/North West) reported in January 2015 that 80 percent of polygraph results are incorrect and that they are not, in fact, lie detector tests, because breathing and heartbeat rates don't measure the truth.[1] In this Colorado case, the guardian was dead set against the mother and the therapists, and he or she had never even met the child. Is this a violation of this child's civil rights? And this family's right to protect their child?

Time and time again, mothers report abuse—and again, specifically sexual abuse on their child. In an unhappy reversal of fortune, the very system designed to protect her victimizes her.

Often the therapist reporting the abuse is discredited and not only at the mercy of one attorney for the child—the guardian *ad litem* (GAL)—and his or her perceptive filters and opinions but also ultimately the decision of the court, a.k.a. the judge. This life-impacting decision then rests ultimately in the hands of one person who is as subject to human errors, perceptions, beliefs, and opinions as anyone else—and yet there it is.

Below is a link to an article revealing the bias of certain courts in certain states regarding mothers who report child sexual abuse. I've seen this happen. Sometimes mothers are regarded as criminals, troublemakers, or liars; they are basically described as hysterical. Often, children are placed with their fathers because that is whom the state pays state and/or federal support to. This article shows how the deck is often stacked against the person who reports, especially the mother, who can be fined or penalized in other ways for trying to get the truth out (http://www.change.org/petitions/stop-the-victimization-of-mothers-reporting-sexual abuse).[2]

Now, there may exist more enlightened states than Alabama, but as a child therapist, I have worked in four states: Colorado, Hawaii, Oregon, and Washington. I have found that the above issue is sadly true with a few rare exceptions. And I will go so far as to call this situation evil, which I define as the extreme end of emotional and spiritual illness.

Years ago when Dr. Scott Peck wrote *People of the Lie*, his work went far to illustrate that there are people who can't see the truth of their unconscious behavior toward children and those who *refuse* to see it. He wasn't afraid to name the evil he encountered as a psychiatrist.[3]

Children are often discriminated against instead of protected. They are subject to adult laws of communication instead of provided proper channels for communication (such as an interpreter for the deaf). And like all discrimination, the ones we call *they* or the ones holding the most social power to justify it.

There is one thing most people forget about those who are out to protect the perpetrator instead of the child or just plain miss essential information due to lack of training. Sooner or later, a child victim is going to find his or her voice and talk. And I can just about guarantee that this generation will clearly speak their truth, and they will be a lot younger than any previous generation. In addition, the truth of their experiences will be posted worldwide for everyone to see. Unfortunately, in the meantime, disrupted development and a negative self-concept, coupled with learning and relationship delays, occur regardless. There is nothing pretty about unhealed sexual abuse, no matter how it manifests later in life.

Let's return to Sarah's representative case. She couldn't talk about her abuse at three and a half, but she could play about her experiences. She had to process the abuse somehow if she was ever going to feel whole again. Although Sarah's behavior and mood improved, she did well enough in school and with her peers, and she seemed to love both her mother and her father. What she was left with wasn't just a very twisted view of marriage; sadly, it will be years before she knows whether she is a "good" or "bad" human being. When Sarah refers to herself or looks in the mirror, she says, "There are two of me." Unfortunately, this response isn't just about seeing her mirror image. Sarah has split apart inside. Like I said, a life-time sentence.

Metaphors of Abuse

Kovi wasn't quite three, and during her first session, she walked right up to the baby bottles and stuck her finger in the nipple. She started an in-and-out motion with the nipple and then undressed the baby. Kovi was five before she was able to win her independence from her father, who sexually abused her. Against all odds and statistics, he confessed—an extremely rare event. Kovi worked on the effects of her abuse off and on for the following three years, but if her father hadn't eventually confessed, I doubt anyone would have believed her story except her maternal family and me.

Many child therapists have witnessed these stories. A similar situation happened involving a little boy too. He wasn't quite three years old, and his father—I hesitate to use the word *father*, as one sperm doesn't a father make—sexually abused him when he was two before the visits with the child became supervised. When I called CPS to report a suspicion of child abuse based on the boy's play criteria, the CPS worker literally (not metaphorically) laughed at me. When the mother reported the same, she was viewed as lying, hysterical, and so on. She wasn't taken seriously, but she was assumed to be trying to ditch a deadbeat, one-night-stand man.

Because of CPS's refusal to believe or even consider a child's traumatic play themes, which were explicit and consistent over time, this child struggled in the playroom off and on for three years and in his life until he was six. Then one day after he left his session, he came back and said he wanted to tell me something. He told me his father had exposed his penis and made him "lick it" when he was a baby. I reported this story to CPS and never heard another thing about it. Sometimes, I am rendered as powerless as the child – thus the book. Anyone who has waited three years or half of his or her life to be believed and validated knows how unjust and crazy this is.

My question is, why do these children have to suffer and struggle for years before their story is heard or, at the very least, given serious consideration as representing the truth? And more importantly, what can be done about it?

I speak not only for the children. There exist thousands of therapists nation-wide, perhaps worldwide struggling to protect children. They face the same frustrations with reporting child abuse, specifically adult-on-child sexual abuse to CPS when very young children make disclosures of abuse through their play themes. Verbalizations sometimes confirm these only years later when the child has attained a new level of maturity.

In general, CPS and the legal system have too often disregarded reports of this nature. Also alarming is child-on-child sexual abuse, and for some unknown reason, this appears to be more easily believed than adult-on-child sexual abuse, which we all know has been going on prior to the Old Testament being written. Probably forever. Human sexuality is oozing out of the very limiting social construction we've tried to squish it into for so long.

I know the world is full of injustice, but attention this one issue has been very quiet. Although it is no longer swept under the carpet, when it comes right down to it, what rarely happens is that the perpetrator is found responsible or given appropriate consequences for his or her actions.

Jules

I'm sure many more efforts have been, and will be made to understand a young child's play themes to obtain the true story of his or her abuse. Every time one adult understands the language of children, we move closer to giving the children an authentic voice.

When a young child like Jules reveals sexual intrusion into her mind, body, and soul, I have to wrestle with the fact that a child just told me through her play that "a mean man comes into my room at night and says and does wrong things," violating all of her boundaries and destroying her dignity for years to come. I have little to no evidence to support her allegations. When Jules referred to her perpetrator as a "robber," the clarity of her metaphor is present in her life, because she has been robbed of her dignity and sense of wellbeing. So at six years old Jules understood this form of robbery. But she used a little monkey as a self-object and showed this little monkey clinging to its mother's back. In about one minute or less, she showed the "mean man" going into the little monkey's room at night.

Jules's birth mother and her boyfriend abused her while she endured visitation over the weekends as a toddler; she was court ordered to spend time with her mother. Most stunning was that she took two babies—her age at the time the abuse started—and put them in the play oven. She then took the role of her perpetrator, who lied to her mother about where she (Jules) was by claiming not to know.

This was Jules's metaphoric play, a profound descriptor of her personal experience as a toddler. Now she has to heal from a volcanically disrupted course of development. At six and in therapy because her grandmother was raising her—the mother and boyfriend seemingly lost interest in her—she told me, "I don't know who I am."

Sadly, Jules isn't even considered a reliable witness; however, children are *always* the first and generally the most reliable witness to their abuse. Of course, it takes a good deal of experience (and?) to show up in court and talk about seriously about a little monkey needing her mother's protection and a "mean man" roasting babies in the oven. It also takes a great deal of courage and faith to present a child's play themes (for consideration of the abuse) as being true in court. I get why this is so, but it's time to start looking at kids' play in a new way.

The facts and statistics related to child abuse are staggering. Research shows that very few children lie about being sexually abused. Data also indicates that most allegations the father brings against the mother are false, but it's not true the other way around.[4] I once had a case that went to the California Supreme Court. The mother had accused the father of molesting their daughter and I had to choose to be her therapist. The case was very scary indeed. I had to figure out whether the father had molested the child while she was in his custody and was then only about six or seven years old. This "play evaluation" went on for over a year. It became clear over time that in this case, the mother was lying to eliminate the father from their child's life. Her truth was revealed in a series of puppet shows where she was able to show the coaching from her mother, the witch who cast spells upon the daughter. The mother's hysterical behavior did not help this child either but served to reveal that this little girl only had sexual issues while visiting her mother's home. That is a report I never want to write again.

So when a child tells a trusted adult, as he or she has been taught to do, and then nothing happens, and the report is rendered almost as powerless as the child, we have a situation.

Judges and attorneys hold an unbelievable amount of power in the lives of children and their parents. Whether they are aware of their sacred contract to protect children, it has been made, or they wouldn't be in such a trusted position. Although some folks become teachers and camp counselors to abuse children, it is becoming more and more evident that some CPS workers, attorneys, and child investigators are negatively motivated as well. I know some good ones still but trusting that justice will be served is pretty difficult.

Once a report has been made to CPS or the police, the child most often continues his or her healing journey with the reporting therapist. Because so much is at stake, these cases can drag on for years. In general during this time, therapists report to the attorneys for both parents and to the child's attorney, who, in turn, reports to the commissioner or judge, who ultimately decides the child's fate.

If a case "goes to trial"—and it is indeed a trial—the involved professional has to testify as the voice of the child, which then has to be translated into "adult" language for the court. Or at least that is what a good child therapist would be willing and able to do: speak for the child. Time and again the child, the supporting parent, and the therapist are put on trial instead of the perpetrator of the abuse; they are accused of "coaching" a child into slandering an adult with false accusations.

Generally speaking, it is the therapist who knows the child. Certainly after spending ten, twenty, or even forty or fifty hours with a child on his or her inner journey, which is both intimate and productive for a child to travel, a trained and effective therapist knows the child's inner world. One question is why the judicial system doesn't have enough respect for the therapist to believe him or her when he or she speaks for the child. Instead, the reporter is put on trial; time and time again, it is the perpetrator, not the child, who is protected.

So when the child's attorney who is hired for basically a lot of money (far more than the therapist makes) to protect a child, makes decisions regarding said child without ever meeting that child, this behavior is a major discounting of the child as a person. These days it seems like too many people, hired to protect children, are more like absent parents. They aren't bad people (are they?) but perhaps too afraid to really protect the child due to fear that the angry parent, who is fighting the parenting plan, will hurt *their* family. Being PC (politically correct) carries a positive intention, but this language is based in fear, not respect.

There are, of course, good guardians who use their legal power to protect a child from harm. These are the attorneys who are actually concerned about the welfare of the child and take the time to conduct a very thorough investigation into the truth of the allegations against someone. It is vitally important that these investigations be completed in a way that protects the person accused of abuse *and* the child but not *instead of* the child.

One aspect of a child's reality, which is easy to spot in the playroom, is his or her use of time. Many children burst into their play and start processing and solving their problems as best they can untangle them. Others hold back but still assess the value and purpose of the room. Some are simply thrilled to find vehicles, games, sand, or babies. Then there are a few children who cannot use their time in a productive way at all and just sort of stall for whatever reason. But in children who have been violated sexually—even if this violation is "just" emotional or psychic—the child's response to the playroom will be a strong indicator of the impact of the violations on the child.

Their play is weird, plain and simple. Any adult witnessing this play would feel the pull of the truth that something is wrong. The play is maladaptive, and the child is silent, avoids eye contact, over engages the therapist, ignores the therapist, breaks toys, identifies with broken toys, or zooms from one thing to another chaotically, almost always showing themes of invasion, insertion, or intrusion and extreme powerlessness.

The very nature of most child investigation is anti-child. The child victim as young as three years old is placed in a room with strangers without the support of the reporting parent to prevent coaching. Strange adults ask this child a series of questions; rarely, if ever, is a child able to confirm either the play themes or verbalizations made to the therapist, whom they know and trust. When perpetrators are interviewed, it should come as no surprise that their best defense is "I didn't do it!" They cry that the reporting parent hates them and is trying to destroy them and take their child away by making up false allegations against them, especially when a highly conflicted divorce is involved. I've often wondered what else investigators expect a child molester to say.

In murder cases this answer would be held as highly questionable, and the investigation would continue. But in cases of child sexual abuse this doesn't necessarily occur, and investigators report finding no evidence to support the report of abuse. And it is soul murder, an emotional death for a child who is essentially called a liar or not given a chance to tell the truth their way. We all know what that invalidation feels like.

There is data to indicate that child sexual abuse has been with humanity since the beginning of time, and it is still sanctioned in many ways and in many places. If you know ten people, approximately three or more of those people will have experienced some form of sexual abuse. The data from ten years ago is startling, and in spite of programs designed to prevent child abuse, nothing seems to really impact human nature bent to be predatory. Child sexual abuse, like rape, is traditionally underreported. Young children rarely disclose verbally and don't respond well to interviews that depend primarily on verbal disclosures. This type of interviewing could prove to be grossly inadequate, even dangerous. [5]

A Course in Miracles teaches that the body is a communication device, and children not only know this but have no choice but to live it. The level of a child's ability to communicate is commensurate with the environment in which that communication is received and the adult's ability to truly enter a child's world and thereby gain his or her trust. It is heartbreaking for a child to clearly show adult-on-child sexual abuse and then experience that the trusted adult to whom the disclosure was made isn't believed because our system is designed to protect the perpetrator, not the child, and because of ignorance of how children really communicate their experiences, both positive and negative.

Professionals who work with children and recognize their spiritual or secular agreement to protect children from abuse are thwarted in their attempts to do so because of the deeply ingrained (if unconscious) belief that children exist to serve adults' whims, compulsions, and fantasies, regardless of the evil and ugly nature of those compulsions. Based on statistics and the resulting findings of investigators, guardians, CPS, and so on, one has to ask who is perpetrating the abuse if so many evildoers go undetected and basically get off scot free while the child suffers for life.

Parents who have witnessed this maladaptive play have experienced jaw-dropping revelations regarding the accuracy of their child's play, which reflected their actual experiences and their subjective feelings regarding those experiences. Investigators who provide at least three sessions with the child in a therapeutic playroom are much closer to getting to the truth from that child then three verbally oriented interviews.

The earliest intervention possible is most likely to positively affect future child sexual abuse in the victim's life. It's like a monkey that clings to your back and stays there for your entire life until you find the magic that makes the monkey disappear or fly away or at least obey. Imagine that.

Child sexual abuse fundamentally confuses children, hurts them, scares them, and bends them in the wrong direction. Children, like trees, grow in the direction they are bent. Child sexual abuse, like all child abuse, bends children's relationships toward the dark side. The very foundation of life concerning issues of trust, safety, truth and lies, love and hate, and good and evil are tainted. People can and do heal from abuse. Life would be truly pointless if we couldn't heal from our wounds. But children who get to tell their story early on and are believed and supported avoid a virtual lifetime of carrying around a wild and crazy monkey.

Child sexual abuse, we now know, is prevalent, is sanctioned (although silently) by our most "sacred" institutions, manifests in a plethora of attitudes and behaviors throughout life, and generally and negatively affects relationships due to feelings of separation and loneliness, coupled with fears of unworthiness and abandonment. Feeling insecurely attached doesn't make for a healthy relationship, because when our emotional needs override everything and everyone else, our lives are trouble.

Years ago, when I was in the initial intensive training to provide play therapy, we were assigned a client to work with every day for a week. The child I worked with had been ritualistically abused, and everyone could see it. He was just barely four years old. He had me tie him in a chair and put food and water in his lap, but he couldn't reach the food because his hands were tied behind his back. Don't panic. I was in his role. I was in the child-sized chair, and he took on the role of perpetrator. I'm reminding the reader that this play was *totally* child led and created. I couldn't believe this was the case I had been given.

He screamed at me, mocked me, and instructed me to cry and say I was hungry and beg to see my mom. He'd call me a "baby, a cry baby!" and tell me to "shut up!" He even played driving to the graveyard and eating flesh. Talk about an initiation into play therapy. Luckily, I had a bug in my ear and Dr. Byron Norton, originator of experiential play as my coach. Feeling the boy's terror, living it in a sense, I knew his experience was real. In his final session, this child completely destroyed the playroom, throwing every toy into a mountain in the center of the room. This was too much to sort through in a week for a four-year-old.

I was horrified and fascinated. What part of the play was true? What had happened to this little boy? I will never know, but this was thirty years ago, and the chill remains when I recall this one. This was a case where CPS was helpful in protecting the child. He was also immediately placed into longer-term play therapy as well as into help with deprogramming.

Professionals who work with children and recognize their spiritual or secular agreement to protect children from abuse are thwarted in their attempts to do so in part because of a deeply ingrained (if unconscious) belief that children exist to serve adults' whims, compulsions, and fantasies, regardless of the evil and ugly nature of those compulsions. Based on the statistics and resulting findings of investigators, guardians, CPS, and so on, one has to ask who is perpetrating the abuse if so many evildoers go undetected and basically get off scot free while the child suffers for life. And all too often, society suffers too.

Children manifest a variety of symptoms, and some deviate from what is considered a range of predictable behaviors, such as nightmares, withdrawal, aggression, sexual perpetration, increased separation anxiety, enuresis, aggression, lying, stealing, overachieving, brutal sports participation, animal cruelty, and so on. These are like all the behaviors you don't want to see in a child. A family member or someone the child knows commits almost 80 percent of child abuse.[6] When we consider the level of damage to all involved and all who radiate out from that dark hub, it may be time to listen more deeply to the children's allegations of harm.

With cases of adult-on-child sexual abuse, children have sometimes reported to their parents, investigators and detective when they were interviewed, therapists, family, and friends that they have suffered abuse, but many are not believed due to lack of evidence or who the accused was. These cases are dismissed on the grounds that the children were coached, but no one ever produces any evidence of coaching. In one case involving two siblings, they were in therapy for several years due to their situations and behaviors before sexual abuse allegations came up. It seems to me that the mother wouldn't have waited that long to report her suspicions, especially since both children had come home from visits with chronic UTIs (urinary tract infections) if she was invested in coaching them to say that.

The one person who really knows what happened to them is the child, who isn't here except in this echo of his or her story. In the case mentioned above, the children won. The judge, a father, gave the children the decision-making power to decide whether and when they wanted to see their father again. Sometimes the truth is revealed, and finally the children can move on.

Years ago during my last hard case in the Rocky Mountains, a young mother came into the office one morning to tell me that she knew her husband had been sexually abusing their daughter for a long time. The daughter was only three years old at the time. This case dragged on for two years and involved many more professionals than me. The case cost the maternal family over $100,000 (and this was in 2005) to prove what we knew to be true after many intense play therapy sessions. It was an extremely complicated case. The father had passed a polygraph and many other "tests" most sociopaths can pass without a problem. The defense attorney tried to rip me and all other professionals on the case to shreds. But in this case, all the defense attorney's red-faced blustering and posing didn't work.

The judge was the father of six children, and this fact most likely saved this child from further abuse. We won—the child won—because the judge knew the allegations of sexual abuse were true. This incredible man actually listened to, considered, and allowed her play themes, her behaviors, and some of her art into the trial as evidence. In the end she, at the age of five, was granted decision-making power as to when and if she ever wanted contact with her father again.

CHAPTER SIX

The Broken Truth

Several years ago, seven-year-old Jewel wrote to me,

> Our earth, that we think is earth, is really the broken truth, not earth. Earth is always green, with fairies, angels. It never turns brown—it's always green there. We live inside the broken truth on this earth. Our people have destroyed earth.
>
> All of the people need to care for and honor our earth—we are inside the broken truth, which is on our real earth. We cannot get to the real earth until we get to the real truth. Real truth is to not build shade.
>
> We need to learn on this pretend earth how to treat the earth and all of its life with love and kindness and what God really put inside of us. Then we will be on the real earth.[1]

Okay, this may sound a little bit like the movie *Being There*, but from the mind of a seven-year-old child, it seems as if Jewel can see heaven on earth. What does she really see, and what is she trying so hard to convey to the world that cannot really hear her? Surely she sees what lies beyond the scope of physical vision by describing our amnesia as to our true home, which is here because this is all there is. Why is it that when someone opens to the prophetic wisdom of children and reads those words, he or she gets truth bumps?

Jewel has not only internalized concepts of right and wrong; it seems that she can see right from wrong with spiritual eyes. Jewel was a typical child in the sense that she certainly might disobey her mother, but the guilt for misbehavior has been deleted from her circuitry. Guilt can serve a healthy purpose when used as a trigger for correction. So a child can possess spiritual eyes with which to see but still commit kiddie crimes, just like a person isn't necessarily kind or wise because he or she possesses psychic or clairvoyant abilities.

What did Jewel mean by the "broken truth"? Now in 2016 over twelve years since I played with Jewel, "broken truth" makes more sense now than it did even then—before the phones and binding contracts took over our lives. Or are trying to.

It isn't easy, even for me, to pinpoint what makes these millennial children different from previous generations. Most are simply bright, young luminaries built for the future and can be very challenging to be with, work with or raise now. What I do know is that we need to understand the children of the millennial generation, connect with them, learn from them, and guide them into a vastly unknowable future that may or may not even exist.

My great-niece was only two and a half years old when she held up her little hand like a stop sign if you tried to speak while she was talking. "I'm talking," she clarified for the adults at the table behind her tiny hand. (Gracie, my great niece, was the four-year-old who wanted to throw my sister under the bus.)

Children have always astounded adults with their spontaneous words and actions, but there have never been so many gifted children on the planet at once; and of course overpopulation dictates not only much of the course of life on the earth but also the changing times for its children. So the competition for resources is fierce; very young children are making money already and gaining command over their world.

What I know is this: we are facing a generation I have labeled the mega-millennial generation that *must* learn to respect authority, and we must be that respectful authority. If those in positions of authority don't learn to enter the world of the child when making decisions about that child's life, and make those decisions from only the adult perspective, too much is lost.

CHAPTER SEVEN

The Price of Assumptions

Five-year-old Kara crept into the kitchen, where her mother and her mother's attorney friend sat in the kitchen, talking and drinking tea as their children played upstairs. Kara kept coming into the kitchen to ask her mother to come upstairs and play with her; her two-year-old brother, Dean; and their two friends, Ellen and Marta.

While the friends innocently chatted with each other, Kara's mother routinely smiled, declined her child's request to play upstairs, and sent her back to play with her friends. Not a shadow of a dark thought crossed her mind. After all, she was a therapist, and her friend was an attorney. It was a bright, sunny day in Colorado, and the four children were friends.

Kara obeyed her mother and retreated back upstairs to play. About half an hour later, Kara returned to tug on her mother's overalls, sort of whining. "Come, Mom. Play with us upstairs." This was unusual behavior for Kara, but still no alarms went off for Rebecca, Kara's mother. "I'm visiting with Rose. Are you hungry?"

Again, Kara silently climbed the stairs. When she returned again to her friends, her big-blue eyes had to see the same scene she was trying so hard to end. Ellen and Marta, four and six years old respectively, had Dean's diaper down around his knees, and they continued to molest him. Over a year later, Kara and Dean were able to tell m, and their parents about their early sexual experience in various ways. Ellen and Marta had learned about oral and manual penile stimulation from someone somehow. Kara and her toddler brother had learned about these acts from them.

Unbeknownst to the adults in their lives, this sexualized play continued for about another six months until Kara turned five and a half years old. Sometime during those six months of development, Kara learned how to protect her little brother but not by verbally reporting to her parents. One day when the kids were "playing the game" again, she stopped them by saying, "Put Dean's diaper back on, or I'm telling!" That was enough to stop Ellen and Marta in their tracks. Kara took Dean by the hand and brought him downstairs, but still she didn't tell her mother what was happening right away.

I received a call from the mother, Rebecca, her voice trembling, just a few weeks later. "We need to set up an appointment for Dean and probably Kara too. Dean has been trying to penetrate Kara from behind. When he is alone, we caught him licking the nipples on Kara's doll. One time Kevin, the children's father, caught him licking it (the doll) between its legs with the doll's dress up over her face. He is only two years old! Where could he have learned this behavior?"

"How's Saturday at ten o'clock?" I asked, inwardly groaning over the ordeal to come. Dean was twenty-six months old when I met him, and the first thing he did was to show me what a good imitator of behavior he was. I squatted down parallel to him to greet him at eye level. He looked me squarely in the eyes and squatted down just like I was; and when I observed, "You are good at imitating people," his smile lit the room.

Without jumping to conclusions, I realize that little Dean had just told me through his body language that what he would show me (and his behaviors at home) was something he'd learned from adults and was imitating. In the beginning, I keep these ideas to myself. After each play communication (described below), the general theme will appear in parentheses.

He led the way into the playroom, followed by his parents, and could barely reach into the sand table because he was so little. Standing on his tippy-toes, he let the sand run through his fingers (feelings of loss), then pushed the bop bag out of his way, and the bop bag was bigger than he was (someone in his developmental way). Then he heaved a big blue plastic truck into the sand and crashed it in the center of the sand table (this is the guy's truck and body—he smashed me right in the center of my being).

I said, "That big blue truck crashed right in the middle of the table and hard!" I had just met this boy in diapers, so I stayed focused on his actions to show him I wouldn't just intrude on his play or make verbal assumptions in his presence. He was working on establishing trust with me, and by my not saying more than ten words or asking questions, this trust became possible for him to develop.

Several weeks of play unfolded. Dean chose a brown baby boy doll and placed him in a swing. This doll is about two inches high. Dean pushed the baby in the swing and cried out, "Ouch! Owie!" Then he said, "It doesn't hurt." He replaced the baby in the swing with the male figure, then placed the man, lying facedown, on the ground with the baby. Then Dean put the baby doll in the back of the big blue truck, traveled to some destination, and arrived somewhere. Dean took the baby from the back of the truck, threw him in the sand, and repeatedly ran the blue truck over the baby. The blue truck was central to Dean's play and true life experience, and it remained remarkably consistent throughout his therapy.

As the reader, you can see how these actions, of course, are subject to interpretation, but after so many therapists have reported the same types of themes associated with specific types of experiences, one should wonder and become more inquiring into his or her own innate ability to communicate. Babies are now learning baby sign language. Since this type of nonverbal communication is easier to believe and work with, babies who learn sign language may be the needed bridge to travel from the adult world into the child's world in the next generation.

An experiential play interpretation of the play described above is this: an adult male hurts a baby boy over and over and tells him, "It doesn't hurt," programming little Dean into the school of denying his own pain. The man has inserted himself into the child's world, shown by replacing the baby in the swing.

Then the man lies down with the baby and takes the baby in his truck (the adult world and the man's body) to essentially use him.

I said, "That baby isn't safe. He should be in a car seat with a seat belt. This guy doesn't know how to take care of a baby." Dean was listening, and his parents sat there with mouths agape. I continue, "He tells the baby things don't hurt when they do. That baby got hurt a lot." He stopped his play to go nurse at his mother's breast, seeking comfort, as my validating words confirmed the reality of his experience.

Several times Dean played with the slinky between his legs, moving it up and down, with his hands making it grow long and large and then small again. He'd lock eyes with me to make sure I got it.

A toddler's brain is as active as an adult's brain. By age three, children's brains are twice as active as adults and stay that way for at least ten years. Kids are not only linguistic geniuses during the first decade; they are primed to learn, period.

Dean didn't have the power of choosing to say no to his experience at age two or of saying no to playing with two little girls, who'd learned about adult sexuality before riding bikes without training wheels. Dean did, however, have the power to communicate what he'd witnessed and experienced. He didn't have a choice about the destructive nature of his experience and how these negative experiences had altered the formation of his brain's development. Brain research shows that though it's great in many ways that the brain is elastic and plastic, it also suggests that there are times when bad experiences have more serious and lasting effects—like in the first three or four years.

Right under the noses of two intelligent and caring women, children in ages four and six years old had abused this little boy and his sister. The next question was, of course, where did they learn about oral sex? What did they see or experience that turned child's play into adult play? Imagine: successful and generally aware mothers enjoying tea in the kitchen but unaware of the emotional soups boiling over just up one flight of stairs. It wasn't until Dean started undressing his sister's dolls and lying on top of them that his play revealed the truth loudly enough to cause questioning and alarm. It took time for Kara and Dean to heal; it took more time for their parents to heal. Needless to say, the father of the girls and their mother were headed towards a divorce.

The truth of this book is that children can communicate at the same level as adults if they are given the tools with which to do so; toys are children's words, and play is their language. The world may be changing, shifting, ending, or transforming; but children are still children and have to experience growing pains, even if they are old souls trapped in small and frustrating bodies and situations. And as children, they still need guidance and support as well as validation and the power to negotiate.

A six-year-old little girl I've known for some time told me about the bullies at her school, consistently naming them one by one and week after week. "Aiden, well, he went over to the dark side; they all did."

"Did you go over to the dark side?" I asked.

"Undecided," she replied as she fought with the lump of black Play-Doh.

She was angry. She detailed her frustration like this: "They say to walk away, but they follow you. They say to ignore them, but they ignore you. It doesn't work! The duties don't do anything to help." The truth is, this child needs empowerment, help, and support, but the bullies need even more help.

In other words, as a rather fragile six-year-old child, she'd tried everything she'd been taught to protect herself from bullies, but she felt powerless and disappointed when she didn't get the support she needed. She really just wanted to play princess. School must address the issue of bullies and educate all children about issues of power and control while adults overcome their own need for power and control.

In some ways, meeting these children every day is often like meeting a movie star. Some of these children exhibit the charisma of a Kennedy and an ability to find loopholes in the rules like J. Edgar Hoover with the observational prowess of Sherlock Holmes himself. They are so bright, so built for the future, that their native, natural evolutionary intelligence overwhelms parents.

If I'm four years old now, I will be eighteen in 2025. I'm willing to bet my savings account that no one can see that far into the future, but I do know that when adults wake up to the fact that children are the way they are so they can stand a chance at surviving in 2025-2030; parenting and adult child communication needs to evolve in order to meet the needs of a changing generation of humans.

CHAPTER EIGHT

More Therapists' Thoughts

Adults and children create collective "my stories" together in an almost indescribable blending of energies, motivations, programming, and best intentions—all overshadowed by soul, social and genetic connections.

The following contains one more story regarding Jewel of the "broken truth." Her mother, Kat, told me this story:

> When Jewel was only four and a half years old, she stood with her hands on her hips and spoke earnestly to me. "Mom," she began, "you sure do have a challenge and a journey raising me." I was a bit surprised by what Jewel was saying to me, and it took a minute to sink in. I only got out, "Yes, I do … ?" Jewel said to me, "Well, Mom, along the way I want you to treat me with dignity." I said, "Okay, but do you know what the word *dignity* means?" And she looked me right in the eye and said: Of course I do, dignity is the strength that holds up your love."

A six-year-old little girl I've known for some time told me about the bullies at her school, consistently naming them one by one and week after week. "Aiden, well, he went over to the dark side; they all did."

Lately, I've been getting calls from parents of children as young as two and a half and three years old. Having a "new crop" of very young clients caused me to rethink some of the things I felt were important to tell parents and professionals. The main difference was to explain my personal position on diagnosing children with disorders or rather *not* diagnosing them as being afflicted with anything other (usually) than being very young children in the twenty-first century and all that it entails.

It isn't that some of these disorders don't exist. Reactive attachment disorder is as real as humanity. The now-called "autism spectrum disorder" including ADHD and Asperger's syndrome is "real"—we don't know why these diagnoses are on the increase, but they are. Certainly a bipolar disorder diagnosis is quite popular now and the one that is real as humanity embraces a host of anxiety disorders. These so-called disorders tend to be over-diagnosed and over-medicated, and they produce increasingly violent or subdued children. It may just be time to start merging more of the thought system of spirit than ego—less competition and more cooperation, less division and more unity, less frantic energy and more rest. No one can define "spirit" in words. The meaning to be conveyed here and throughout this book is that spirit equals awareness or consciousness and that this awareness needs to be applied to each one of us to acknowledge our unity, our sameness – that we all share the same humanness. If we were to be invaded by aliens would we join as one?

When freed from illusions, we know how to heal ourselves and our planet knowing that as truly human beings we are flawed but not disordered. The world itself may have been designed to feel like something is disordered to bring us one degree closer to what is real and true, not unreal and false- which is everything temporary. Labeling a child as disordered is pretty heavy, really. What is true for most children struggling to any significant degree with the educational status quo is, for example, showing that it's the child's learning environment is the key to finding the true "diagnosis." When children are placed in the correct learning environment, many "disorders" disappear or significantly reduce.

Children in general must look out at their world and wonder whether they can trust the adults who created such a mess. Could this account for some of the defiance and disrespect? Even if we are the most environmentally conscious vegans, are we not part of the problem if we don't treat our children with the respect we want in return? Are kids just withdrawing into themselves? Is the issue the lack of nutrition in commercialized farming and food? Is embracing a problem just a way to escape the overwhelming energy of the world? Is there more to this problem of increasing "disorders" than meets the eye? Are we just recognizing these symptoms more often? Do we just want to medicate kids? Do we want to change the kids rather than the effort it takes to change ourselves and their environment? Or do we just love labels because labeling appears to make life more manageable and we can pretend we are in control.

Children need to be recognized for having qualities that will help them survive in an unknowable, unforeseeable future instead of being instilled with the belief that they are "disordered," bending the "my story" in a potentially negative direction. It is the world that is disordered, but collectively we can change the direction of the world, and this task starts with everyone, including children, having basic rights without a fight. This is not the right to sue their parents but the right to be heard because *they are us*! We have to validate their empowerment and personal life force, and bend them toward the light.

This is contrary to what we've been taught to believe about children for time and eternity—that tragic events, divorces, deaths, bullies, and so on don't really affect children and that they will "get over it." Examine your own life; have you gotten over these issues yet? There are no deeper imprints than the ones made in childhood, and none are more lasting.

Based on the current level of violence in the world, I think we need to reconsider our position on childhood. Current research indicates that kids' brains may develop differently now than when we were children. Children have more choices and too much information; they are expected to make quick decisions hundreds of times a day. There is more stimulation to the more primitive parts of the brain, and this, in turn, affects the development of the frontal lobe—or the seat of emotions, that which makes us human. This very young generation appears to be way ahead in areas of cognition, being able to "read" people and situations, even to be creative problems solvers at times; but this generation is so unbalanced by overload in certain parts of their development that their emotional selves become stuck and overwhelmed.

Economic and paradigm shifts affect everyone; hurricanes, floods, fires, and other natural disasters rock our very planet. I know children who lose sleep worrying about the safety of the animals inhabiting the earth. One little girl had to "play" rescuing the animals and environment before she could relax enough to fall asleep and stay asleep; she was only eight years old! Her solution was to ask every family to plant at least one tree.

The way to respect the "new kids" is to validate that their demand for perfection isn't a "disorder," but it may well be a necessary adaptation to live in a future world we adults cannot even envision. Maybe that's why so many children with so-called learning disorders can't learn in a traditional school system. It appears that the environment is disordered when children who cannot or will not conform to traditional learning environments learn quickly and easily when they are homeschooled or given an environment that is a match.

We must literally get down on our knees when our children are small and willingly, lovingly, and supportively enter their world of play. Within that world, we need to validate their intelligence and courage, and we need to dot every *I* and cross every *T*. When we give children this respect, this validation, the relationship improves. It is vital to talk to your children about why they have "so much power" and how important it is to learn to use it cooperatively and positively with kindness. As adults, we cannot get to what's positive through what's negative.

More and more often, children come into the playroom and actually show the division between the child world and the adult world that still exists. Children still inhabit an experiential world that has to be experienced to be known. Adults live in a cognitive world, where life can be thought about and decided upon from the couch or the iPhone.

At one point, I worked with a little boy of about two and a half years who went fishing with his uncle and father; he caught his first fish. He spent several sessions processing the opposite energies of the fun of catching a fish with the violence of hurting the fish and then trying to reconcile that with how good the fresh fish tasted. More and more, children have "monsters" under their beds at ages nine—even up to thirteen. The fear is inside them, fostered by the belief in competition in a scary world. Dealing with children's fears and behaviors require a new form of teaching or discipline. Getting to the truth of a child's experience requires a new form of inquiry than in the past. Plain and simple, with few exceptions, the systems of discipline and information gathering are part of an old structure of relating to children in an authoritarian still that will not work. The best teacher is your own example of having self-control and understanding their position in human history. Awareness is the most powerful agent of change we have at our disposal as human beings. If truth is truth on all levels, consider that current research in physics confirms that consciousness creates reality. So keep on imagining a viable future.

I got a call a few weeks ago from a former client, whose eleven-year-old son, Christopher, had a complicated history with his father. He had just returned from his every-other-week visit with his father and stepmother. This child had finally accepted the fact that his father and his new wife had adopted a boy child, who now lived and reigned in the household and was much younger than Christopher. Christopher's father had spent months trying to convince Christopher to leave his mother's country nest, his life, his school, and his friends; and move in with him and his wife and son. Christopher didn't want to change his life; he was happy with things as they were and tried in vain to tell his father this along with help from his mother. Finally, Christopher's father told him that he was paying a lot of child support and that if Chris lived with him, he wouldn't have to pay it; plus he offered better schools and had just moved into a $650,000 house during a major recession.

Okay. Well, Chris came in for just one session. In that one session, he was able to process that he had the right to stay in his life—with his home, his mom, and his friends—and not feel guilty. He could see the misguided nature of his father's request and actually feel some compassion for his father. He still wrestled a little with some need for his father's approval but not much.

When parents come to me with incredibly angry three-year-olds, I have to tell them what I see. There's something in the relationship that just doesn't work for their little child, who has the power to disrupt the entire household. And she does when she angrily demands that things be her way or else; this behavior is actually designed for the redoing of an action to make it right, just being totally defiant, often in a very good family. This behavior will cause the parents to take action. It is a teaching opportunity if the action is positive and consciously recognized as a teaching moment.

I recently met a young, successful couple. They have a little one who urinates on the floor when "pissed!" Then, when the storm passes, she collapses into a heap of despair on the floor and needs to be hugged. Then she doesn't let her mom hug her or demands that only Mommy do it – hug her – while rejecting her father's affections. Very messy to undo.

I once met a family who came in, reporting that their eight-year-old, Karen, was having "rages or storms" that lasted up to three or four hours in the family room. As her mother told me that they had taken everything but her mattress out of her room, chills went up my spine. I wasn't sure whether I should take this child or these parents as a client. I told her mother to put everything that was safe and couldn't cause harm back into her room ... such as scissors and maybe the mirror. I said to return everything for now. The mother went on to describe how the girl's father was on one side of the door while their frantic child pushed in the opposite direction to get out. Their home life was intolerable.

I was aghast but felt the usual therapist's sense of responsibility to do what I could to help. Frankly, I was afraid; I'm prone to have an overactive imagination, and I kept getting flashbacks from *The Exorcist.* Twenty–six sessions later, which consisted of individual and family sessions, the storms passed, and their daughter returned to a happy life.

I will always attribute some of this success to a local, busy child psychologist who didn't "diagnose" Karen but instead informed the parents that her behavior was a parenting issue (to put it mildly). But they listened and followed up on his referral to me. The doctor could have easily sedated this young girl, but he didn't. Here is a small example of their parenting style:

"Well, for example, she would ask for an ice cream cone, and we would say no, and that would bring on a 'storm' that might last for hours." But this is how these parents reasoned. If Karen wanted ice cream, they said no, and she threw a fit, they figured she had suffered enough by not getting the ice cream and completely overlooked the fit.

This is a small sample of the reasons why parents seek therapy for their child and support for themselves. Feeling reassured about this generation's abilities and traits is helpful to most parents.

This family was in a huge emotional uproar and crisis simply because the parents didn't know how to discipline their child and totally misinterpreted her behavior. I mean, they were way off. Heavily Christian in orientation, Karen's mother spoke in spooky terms during the intake, which is saying a lot. I wasn't so sure I could perform the exorcism she and her family apparently needed. But allowing Karen to do her thing in her way and at her level healed the whole family.

Adults have the power to say no, and what we say no to in our lives literally defines our realities. An absolute "no"s provide structure to our inner and outer walls, ceilings, and floors—defining boundaries for expectations, values, and behaviors. Then there are maybes or usually I don'ts, and these are like the windows or doors; they open and closed. It was time to help this family sort out some of these reality creating structures.

By the time Karen's parents came to see me, they told me that all that remained in her room was a mattress and a dresser. Her father had used his body to keep the wild child contained in her dreary prison of a room when she was sent to time-out. By now, it might have been clear that time-out wasn't working and generally doesn't really teach anything to children (using it to calm them down is its best function). The new kids resent being isolated from their families because they could not control their emotions and behavior and were probably imitating the adult behavior they see. Time out doesn't work anymore unless the child chooses it.

As I fought visions of Regan in *The Exorcist*, but I agreed to take this child as a client. I instructed her parents to explain to Karen that they were going to start over as a family. I suggested that they contact their pastor to bless the house and to at least symbolically cleanse it of the haunting fear echoing through the psyche (and mouth) of their child.

Karen often drew pictures of the "twins that live inside of me." They were frightening, hollow images that unnerved all the adults who saw them. I coached her mother to see that we were going to help the twins because they felt scared and were a creation of Karen's dual identities and need for integration within herself and her family. "Look where they live, in the void and hollow place, a haunted place. See how unpredictable children can be? Give them everything but effective and fair discipline, respect, and boundaries; and see what you get."

What became revealed was that Karen's parents catered to her but also judged her. She wasn't the picture-perfect little girl they had imagined escorting to church. One never knew when a storm would rise up and blow the whole family away. She was an "out picturing" of terror - a metaphor in the world of form; in the material world of her inside emotional climate of their failure as parents to teach her the limits and boundaries of life as a child. Karen took twenty-eight experiential play therapy sessions to turn herself around and become a typical child again, attending Scouts and other activities with her peers and treating adults respectfully without fear of participating in life. And learning to accept that sometimes, her parents might say "no" to ice cream.

Her storms ceased completely. All hail to the child psychiatrist who wouldn't give this child a neurological disorder or severe diagnosis. He had the courage to correctly diagnose poor parenting, thus saving her from the further distraction of unnecessary medications and the roller-coaster ride that ensues.

CHAPTER NINE

Todd's Story of Military Deployment and Two More Views

Todd was six years old when his father was sent to the (back then) Gulf War. Todd had to settle for snatches of telephone conversations with his daddy and watch the war on TV which is a horrifying thought in itself. He had a sibling, a younger sister and a lonely, overwhelmed mother. Todd carried a lot of tension in his body, fearing for both of his parents' wellbeing as well as his own and his sister's. Soldiers miss birthdays, holidays, first steps, graduations, new babies, and deaths. Marriages can crack under the strain of deployment. Sometimes the soldier never returns home.

Todd solved his anxiety by becoming a pirate and building a time machine. This inventive six-year-old built (time and time again in many sessions) a time machine out of large cardboard bricks. Inside, he hid the treasure box to keep it safe from the rubber knife (intimate hurts and fears) he used to stab at the bricks. (He built a safe place out of his time machine and showed the threats attacking his feelings of security with the knife.)

After filling his time machine with treasure, he said, "I'll take more of the treasure out. They're pirate coins. They tell me not to put my hand in the machine. I'll get burned." The confusing loss of his father to war threatened his self-worth. Todd was in rebellion to authority because he felt he'd been robbed of his father's love, having it literally pirated away. He created a metaphor of needing gas for his time machine to show his need for fuel or energy to face his new life without his father and all the changes his family was experiencing. Because his home felt dark and lonely without his father, Todd acted out his feelings of powerlessness.

Todd's process of building and rebuilding and being in the time machine symbolized his need to transcend time and space to "be" with his father. His play enabled him to deal with the anxiety he felt in his body. It was as if he were showing me how his own unique soul system had transformed energy from fear to hope inside himself his way. Talking through his creative play, Todd said it was hard to change and overcome his developmental challenges, especially without his father.

When Todd set up the time machine, he created controls he called the "sands of time." He created a control for the past, the present, and the future. Using his gears, he made the past bigger and then moved back into the present. His father existed in the past. Todd spent a lot of playtime moving back and forth through time and space, recapturing times when his whole family was together in the past to trust that they would be together again in the future. Happily, this family got to welcome their soldier home. Pretty soon after the return of his father, Todd didn't need his time machine anymore.

Two More Playroom Views

Her tiny eyebrows arched, and a serious frown let me know that 1-2-3 Magic felt like an insult to my three-year-old.

Words from a frustrated new mother

Children used to look up to their parents. Now they cast them sideways glances. (Author's words)

Eric

My teacher called my mom, who called the principal, the school counselor, and some lady who likes to play with kids; Mom said she had a room full of toys. Sounded like someone told my mom to say that to me so I wouldn't think we were going to see a counselor.

I was ten that summer—well, almost ten anyway. Yay! Summer! I didn't like my fifth-grade teacher; he was bor-ing. I was playing Xbox and getting to a higher level when I heard my mom talking to my dad, who lives in Colorado. Sounded like she was shipping me off for the month of July. Sounds like time to press for a phone because I'll be alone in airports, and, well, things might be looking up. "Mom?"

So, this lady does have an awful lot of toys, way more than me, and lots of stuff to do: games, darts, art—I don't know, music. Anyway, I found this Playmobile dude who reminded me of my dad, so I took him off the shelf and buried him in the sand. The lady said, "Sometimes you can't see this guy." She was right. Most of the time I don't get to see my dad, and I miss him, and I worry about him. He was so sad when my mom left; this makes me angry at her. I say, "I hate you!" to her and then I run to my room and mess thing up, and sometimes I break things. I don't really hate her, I don't think.

So, this lady is nice, and she writes some stuff down, and I ask her what she is writing, but I only ask with my eyes. But she answers me anyway. "I'm writing what you are playing because what you are playing is important. Besides, it's my job to write stuff down."

Okay, fair enough.

So, I unbury the cop that I covered in sand, and she said, "Oh, here he is, back again; now we can see him again." And that's just like what happened the other day with my mom and dad—and just like my dad popping up and disappearing unexpectedly. He makes me nervous; they both do. I wonder why we can't just hang out and do fun things together—no big deal. But it's always a big deal, like he couldn't hold himself up without me by the time he gets around to seeing me.

Sometimes he's cool, and we play games and eat cheeseburgers and fries, but sometimes he yells at his phone and gets all nervous and drives out of control. Man, I don't want to tell her that, but as I zoom this Matchbox car around wildly in the sand, she says, "That guy looks really out of control." Is she reading my mind?

I found a little girl doll and buried her. *Bye, Mom*, I thought all to myself. So the nice lady with x-ray eyes says, "Now, we can't see *her* anymore." I don't think she can read my mind, but I don't want to get my dad or my mom in trouble, just in case.

So, I ask if I can "make a craft." That's safer for today.

Aggie

I was pretending to be a princess because my daddy left me, and my mommy is home all alone by herself. I told my dog, Pal, all about this, but he just looked sad too. The toy lady (I call her Victoyia) said something about the little fairy girl wanting to fly away from the scary dragon, and I thought she was pretty smart for an adult. I think she knew how much I needed to go to Fairy

Land; how much I needed to pretend that everything was all right and that my mommy wasn't going to cry and yell at me every night and then later say she was sorry. I'm afraid my night-light will go out; I am scared of the dark. I think I'll run as fast as I can to Mommy's bed.

CHAPTER TEN

LGBTQ Children and All Garden Varieties

"Sometimes I say I'm a girl; sometimes I say I'm a boy. Sometimes I want to wear a dress or a football jersey. The real question is: 'Does it really matter?'"

It's hard enough to see why someone would choose to experience gender identity as different from gender assignment at birth or to choose to be gay or any other situation that makes life even more of a struggle than it already is. As a therapist, why would any one report a suspicion of child abuse without truly suspecting that abuse? Frankly, reporting such suspicions only adds to the workload and stress for the therapist, sometimes more than anyone can imagine. This may be a poor analogy to gender but nevertheless, when things are just plain challenging being the way they are, it is wise to question the doubts and prejudices regarding the issue not to mention the motivation behind what us humans do. Besides, whether changing gender or sexual identity involves a choice in someone's life or not the truth of who we are seems to threaten our definition of being a good human. Humans contain all qualities that humans display. Simply, the square pegs do not fit in the round holes no matter how much we want them to.

All research strongly indicates that the different ones are born that way; not only that, but trends suggest that that what we've called "normal" is fast becoming the "new different" or a new abnormal.

Accepting the new paradigm of our world indicates a demand to recognize a fresh, advanced generation who are witnessing more people in theory having the rights that everyone on earth is entitled to, and yet so many fighting for equal rights daily. This is especially true for the gender creative, gender nonconforming, and gender curious and people of color. I prefer the term "gender fluid" and will stick with that term. This is still true for children culturally or otherwise different and sadly for any child who cannot use adult language to talk about what he or she has endured. Yes, in many ways, childhood and children remain the same, but the truth is— as the world turns inside out what we fear and misunderstand has to be approached and understood.

When Jeremy came to therapy, he was eight years old, a child of color with a mother without that color. She lived with him as a single mom; his father had "disappeared" (child's words). From the moment he entered the playroom, Jeremy dove into the dress-up clothes, obviously delighted with his find. Each and every time he came to a session, Jeremy dressed as a girl and happily swished and swayed in the playroom in the dresses he found. His mother watched from behind a one-way mirror, jaw loose, eyes wide. The critical moment of choice as to how to respond to Jeremy confronted her. At the time, this gender-creative child was considered to have a disorder and challenged his mother's ability to accept him with unconditional love. Jeremy showed up about twenty years ago when my understanding of gender-creative children was limited, but we both knew enough to accept Jeremy as he was.

In five minutes or five sessions, this parent had to choose between fear and judgment (or fear *of* judgment) and love and acceptance toward her only son, who needed to be her daughter. Anger toward the absent father surfaced, and we had to work through Jeremy's revelation with a lot of love and support. I knew little regarding gender issues with kids at that time, but I knew that without her support, her child's life would be unbearably difficult and lonely. This mother stretched herself in every way until she (actually quickly) accepted what Jeremy had been able to tell her in a way that had seemed blocked before the playroom experience. After about five sessions, she asked me, "Should I go buy him some tights and a dress or what?"

I said, "Better ask Jeremy."

As adults, we always need to ask ourselves these vital questions: What are we teaching the children we come into contact with? How much longer will a small group of so-called normal people decide for everyone else what is acceptable and what isn't? I can tell you right now that there are a lot of adults who are fighting for all children to have equal rights, and in ten years or less, these very young people are going to be shaking the world's antiquated belief structure completely apart—they already are.

I'm no prophet, but it seems clear that soon being normal will be different; what is now viewed as different, deviant, abnormal, or unknown will be the norm. From a spiritual point of view, there is a purpose and a season for everything. The argument that "God doesn't make mistakes" is used to support opposite belief systems regarding the new wave of gender and other experiences, just as warring nations both believe that "God is on our side." The argument of nature versus nurture rages on in spite of evidence showing that humans are born who they are and that adults either mess with that or help that nature to grow in a healthy, positive way. That we have to declare in words that "black lives matter," is a travesty. Would anyone dare to say "white lives matter?" When it's been the white lives mattering too much that has caused so many problems and by white I mean a state of mind in which one uses power over another to feed their ego's needs.

As trite as it sounds, love is the only cure. I want to ask that even the most religious of people, who hate their children because of the way they are born, to revisit the question of unconditional love. I want to ask that we stop turning God into a human being who has fears and hate inside for any humans. These children are here to illustrate that our internal experiences override the man-made conventions of morality and conformity. Let's not crucify them the way we crucified Christ, who came to show us that the ego does indeed crucify us. I've always wondered why the focus isn't more on the resurrection. It seems our times are longing for us to resurrect from the notion of killing, doing violence, and crucifying what we don't understand or those we fear due to ignorance and assumptions. The more we, the adults, protect and guide our children, the more we protect and guide our planet, ourselves and our collective future.

The issues of nature versus nurture are apparently rising to the surface in a new and unprecedented way. Nature decides, and nurture develops and then, we decide. People are born the way they are for a reason, and judgments and discrimination hold us back to the point that we need to choose enlightenment or return to the darkest of dark ages, ignoring the fact that the world is round, that breast milk is better than formula, and that the earth revolves around the sun (to put the issue in metaphoric terms). The only answer as to why we haven't moved past the basic challenges of human rights, the end of wars, and comfort and safety for all begs the question of who is in charge. Admittedly, the ego and spirit don't share the same thought systems, Gender fluid children often seem to possess two spirits, both male and female and just may be here to shed light on our perception of what it means to be human if the rest of us would challenge our programming and fears and just let them. Simply put, we need to change the focus of where we place our attention in the world.

This is a most important question, and I'm sure the vast majority of people are asking themselves, *Who are these people deciding who has rights and who doesn't?* There really is no separation between church and state; there never has been, and it's getting worse. (Which is why churches should pay taxes or stay out of women's bodies and gay marriages and so on—they should at least pay the fair share to engage in legislation that affects people's daily lives.) There is, however, a huge separation between the powerful and the powerless. The microcosm *is* the macrocosm, and by empowering the young ones in a positive and healthy way, we empower everyone. How do we teach our children to be kind and generous when future economic forecasts predict that within a generation, 50 percent of the world's wealth will be in the pocket of the infamous 1 percent. This really doesn't leave enough for the rest of us, regardless of color, gender, sexuality, religious beliefs, and so forth.

This state of affairs is evident by the push for religion to be used as a reason to deny services, recognition of marital unions, and the obtaining of and keeping of employment and so on to the LGBTQ community, which we all know is unconstitutional at the very least. We as humans lack basic trust in life, and if God isn't life, I don't know what is. Trust is the key to freedom. Defining God and believing some are the chosen people are the problem. I grew up with the saying "Many are called, but few are chosen"; what I believe is that we are all called, but few answer.

Since there are gender fluid children who seem to know who they are from toddler age, we need to trust that this is not only how it is but that there is a reason that "all this" is coming to light. So, using language, legislation, and the power to fight about who has rights and who doesn't, how do children stand a chance? Let's face it. Harmful-to-others legislation is based on certain powerful groups who proclaim to know whom God loves and whom God judges as wrong or sinful. The new ones won't tolerate this old way of thinking; they are too evolved, but in the meantime, they have to live in a world full of ignorance and fear.

I didn't learn about consciousness until the infamous 1960s. I didn't learn quantum theories regarding the discoveries that consciousness creates reality, and not the other way around, until this past decade (although some of us always knew this.) My programming was deep, dark, and devious. I wept over *Uncle Tom's Cabin* in spite of the fact that I lived with a hateful mother who was full of fear and bigotry. The seeds of complexity are planted in childhood. It has been the children who have helped me unravel the dark tangle of threads that lead to the light. Consciousness creates reality; keep on pondering that.

I went to Catholic school from age four and a half until twelve. When I was six and in second grade, I sat on the toilet one day and thought (forgive me, Lord), *Even the pope shits.* You can see by this one thought alone that I was always in trouble during my elementary school years. It's been years since I've been involved in a religion of any sort, but I love the new pope; he is progressive, and he gets it—advising people not to waste time worrying about whom people love and sleep with while tossing off the gaudy presentation of God's so-called representative on earth. Our earth needs healing; it isn't too late if we would collectively take a fresh look at life who is being born, and the messages they send us, whatever "too late" might mean maybe we can beat it.

Greed and self-righteousness aren't the only driving forces behind unjust legislation affecting everyone and the current generation's unique challenges. Presuming to be the moral compass for others and deciding what is sinful or not drive all the legislation blocking gay marriage and workplace rights, the gay, lesbian, bisexual, transgender, gender fluid or creative, questioning or queer (LGBTQ) community rights and, to this day, the rights of any oppressed group of people or just anyone stripped of their power of choice and freedom. If religious beliefs of moral superiority don't motivate this, then what will? Jesus himself preached against self-righteousness and the danger of judging others. Not only that, but the story has it that he rose from the dead. So might we, if we open our minds to the idea of an ongoing consciousness, see time as an opportunity to heal and become the co-creators we are gifted to become. We need to rise from the dead and collapsing constructs of everyday life.

When we engage in these debates, the simple and profound issues of respect and kindness are basically buried under a pile of emotional and legislative garbage. The children aren't missing a thing by being so observant and ever so sensitive; they bring crucial issues into our collective face. We have better things to do than to understand children, don't we? Often we hold the keys in our hands, even as we search for them. Seeing the world through another's perspective is all it takes; why are we so not into doing this?

I'm grateful that many, many people on the planet strive to be here in the moment, where the doorway to eternity creaks open and the new kids walk through. If consciousness creates reality, let's join with the children and create a new world for them (who are us).

Adults need to commit to work even harder with the powerful qualities of awareness and intelligence so many children possess. Their strength, persistence, brilliance, awareness, sensitivity, and emotional and nurturing needs—and even their sometimes confounding determination—need to be revisited to quash the disrespect and defiance prevalent in the now generation. Then these super powered children need to be shown how they can exercise their might, which is survival based without expressions of violent anger evident in daily shootings, bullying, or bearing crushing depression. These behaviors are evident in school refusal, suicides, and daily and hour-long meltdowns—when all most children want is true connection.

> What Children Know
>
> As recently as 2014, New York School districts have declared that it is up to the child to declare their gender and take care of nature's call in that bathroom. It is not for schools to decide what gender a child is.[1]

I have worked with very young children who know they are gay or that their bodies are "mixed up." They have to struggle with the issue of which darn bathroom to use at school and at other public places. I'll tell you—look at the gender signs for bathrooms people use at schools and other public places. I'll tell you—take the gender signs off the doors and place a "Unisex Restroom" sign on the doors of public bathrooms so children and others are not discriminated against, taunted, or judged by simply having to engage in a basic biological function. Or just have three bathrooms: "Men," "Women," and "Who Cares?" While we're at it, let's place changing tables in all the bathrooms; these would assist parents of any gender. Moms aren't the only ones who change babies anymore.

Research indicates that the rights of transgender people stand about where the rights of gays and lesbians were in the 1980s. It may be the children who influence society regarding transgender and gender-creative people. These issues are becoming more pervasive and important. How do we change views of why these changes are occurring to preserve the rights of all children?

I believe creation and evolution are inseparable and that evolution *is* creation; consider this concept. Overpopulation is one of the biggest problems on the face of the earth, and everyone knows it or, at the very least, feels it. Could the emergence of people who are unable to reproduce (so far) be an evolutionary adaption to control the escalating numbers of humans who need resources as basic as food and shelter? Could this be a way to provide more homes for the children already here? Is the so-called norm being challenged to review what it means to be human now?

In the same way that biracial marriages appeared to produce some of the most beautiful, intelligent, and strong human beings, we, the adults, are going to have to quickly tap-dance into new ways of thinking with as much grace as possible. It is apparent on a daily basis that things are changing at a more rapid rate than the general population's ability to adapt to those changes. Accepting that people are born the way they are born (nature) and that nurture then becomes the interweaving influence would be a major step toward tolerating and understanding or simply accepting what is and trusting that there is a reason. Trust is the key to freedom.

I've always wondered why groups who believe in ethnic cleansing, for example, never notice that their violence is reprehensible, disgusting, and worse than the dirt they imagine they are cleansing. Who, me? Judgmental? I always wondered why right-to-lifers have no problem sending the fetus they saved to become cannon fodder for some old guy's bank account a mere eighteen years later when we send them off to war. Basically, the human ego can justify any behavior it wants to engage in, all the while adroitly lying to itself. When will we turn off our TVs and computers, and wake up to the underlying truth that propels us each day?

After playing therapeutically with children who, from the age of two years, know that their bodies are "mixed up" or have been sexually or otherwise abused but are unable to talk about this abuse directly, I became even more convinced that children possess an awareness than can be expressed productively and accurately given the correct environment in which to do so and the correct consciousness to observe their play. I have played with gay kids who knew from early on—prior to age five—that they were gay, transgender, and gender-creative kids. Some children seem to possess the wisdom of the ancient wise ones, combined with the clarity and innocence of childhood, in a very cosmic and holy way. Why are we not simply curious about gender, about our beliefs? Why do we feel so threatened?

If we believe "God doesn't make mistakes," then let's believe that and just nurture the children and help to raise awareness and consciousness regarding humanity and its garden variety of expressions. Stop being offended by external differences. Inside, we are all one and the same, globally speaking; we are all in the same boat. Granted, some are in yachts, and some in rowboats, but we are at least in the same waters, and we all want them clean, don't we? I don't know if "god" makes mistakes or not but I know people sure do.

Transgender people, gay people, and the different ones are here to challenge our deepest beliefs about humanity and to show us that the body is secondary to the spirit. In Native American culture, people of this nature were referred to as "two spirit" and were highly respected. In India men have traditionally dressed as women as a normal part of their culture to dress men and women in a similar fashion.

Genetics may well be our spiritual inheritance, and the Xs and the Ys of genetics are creating a new alphabet of language and people as an opportunity to turn from hate to love; from ignorance to understanding; and from slamming the door shut to opening new ones. When a five-year-old child can come to rest for a bit by saying, "I'm transgendered; I'm special," she has found a small island of respite for what perhaps is to come in her life. What I do know is that, although her parents accept her for who she is and totally support her journey into the female, they sure as hell aren't guilty of being possessed by a pathology that would cause this inner conflict in their child. Ironically, the transgender children I have met are generally amazingly charismatic.

In an effort to de-disorder people, different approaches have been taken in the new DSM-V (Diagnostic & Statistical Manual) and by state laws governing the rights of people to decide for themselves who they are.

> House Bill 2451: State of Washington: 63rd Legislature 2014 Regular Session: An Act Relating to restricting the practice of sexual orientation change efforts; amending RCW 18.130.020 and 18.130.180; and creating a new section.

The main issue here is that therapists in Washington State (at least) are prohibited from engaging in conversion therapy or basically forcing children to act in accordance with their biological body instead of the feeling inside. Most current research shows that forcing children to identify with their biologically given body rather than the feeling of gender is more likely to cause harm and psychological damage than honoring the children's belief and experience of their gender. When involved with a highly contentious divorce, the parent who upholds the biological gender of the child tends to still win more parenting time while demonizing the more supportive (of the child) parent. This is another venue of divorce the legal system would be well appointed to further educate itself about. I haven't even mentioned the medical system. There are too many pediatricians who are totally ignorant of gender fluidity, hormone blockers, hormone therapy, as well as behaviors, challenges, and needs of a growing population.

In February 2011, a transgender girl named Coy Mathis was diagnosed with gender identity disorder, a diagnosis the American Psychiatric Association last year removed from the DSM-V list of mental disorders. Without rewriting the online news article, suffice it to say that Coy was in love with pink by five months old and was the biological male of two (triplets) sisters who were biologically female. This type of knowledge early on appears to suggest at the very least that we don't really know a whole lot about being human. During this case, the transgender Legal Defense and Educational Fund planned to explain a ruling by the Colorado Civil Rights Division that allowed Mathis, a six-year-old, to use the girls' bathroom. [2]

As to the most recent debate regarding establishing separate educational facilities for the LGBTQ community of kids, there are two sides or more to the debate. It appears that no one is for absolute "segregation" of the gender fluid youth. Every adult in public and private sectors is faced with how to responsibly and fairly handle bullying, taunting, disclosing or coming out, facing our own programmed prejudices, and having to rethink everything we know about biology and humanity. While we see that segregation isn't the goal, consider this: because this is a new challenge school administrators, teachers, and counselors, in particular, must face, providing an educational option for one or two days a week (by student choice) for the next five years would offer a bridge of time for educating adults and children about how to adapt to what may be evolutionary changes we simply don't comprehend. I think the goal, the intention, is that with education and experience, all children will be seen as true equals and model respectful behavior so separation or the misguided idea of segregation doesn't occur.[3]

CHAPTER ELEVEN

What Siblings Know

When Buddy was four years old, his mother brought him to therapy to help him deal with an outrageous amount of jealousy toward his sibling infant sister. (I chose this story from years ago because more and more children resent the birth of a sibling; it's that competition for attention and resources.) Although it appeared that Buddy "had it all," he was fraught with a deep insecurity; the one thing Buddy lacked was an essential sense of self. He was on probation at preschool! (again)

When his mother was pregnant, he deleted messages from the answering machine, especially regarding prenatal doctor appointments. He hit his parents, pushed other kids, urinated on the floor, spit at people, and engaged in any over-the-top expression of anger and fear he could come up with.

Buddy was cute and super-smart, but he had a screw loose somewhere. Like many children bearing the dubious recognition for being "gifted," Buddy was deliriously happy when content, filled with curiosity and a passion for life. He was in love with travel and adventure, and he was described on the positive side as "developing deep relationships with his family and friends as well as possessing a strong sense of justice." When his mother was in her final trimester and ordered into bed rest, Buddy was enrolled in a cooperative preschool with a wonderful reputation and a long waiting list. But Buddy's take on this plan was simply a feeling of rejection and separation. After his sister was born, he tried to kill her by strangulation, so that's how his therapy got started.

When I first met Buddy, I had already developed the practice of writing play therapy notes while the children were playing as much as possible. In his first session, Buddy asked what I was writing. (Now most kids just ask with their eyes.) I replied that I was writing what he played because it was important. He repeated that he didn't want me to write down what he was playing, so I told him it was my job to do so.

He asked, "Who is your boss?" I was sitting in a grade school–sized chair at eye level with Buddy.

I replied, "I'm the boss."

He quickly surmised, "Then you don't have to write." Checkmate.

The goal of therapy for Buddy was to turn his fear and aggression toward his family and sister into the rightful position of being their child and her protector. To achieve the unspoken but agreed-upon goal, Buddy created a "monster," using me as the monster to express his primal rage to out-picture his fears. Once he confronted the fear that his parents didn't love him, which had turned him into a little monster, his fears slowly subsided.

Some therapists have had the experience of sword fighting or being cast in the role of perpetrator or, in this case, a monster for fifty minutes, and I just want to say it's exhausting work. Even though Buddy took breaks to sing "Folsom Prison" by Johnny Cash, he worked to destroy the monster within through me for twenty-seven sessions. By the time Buddy was able to slay his inner monster, my throat was raw from all the primal growling and howling he directed me to express for him. But his fears subsided, and in the meantime, he taught himself to read, partly because he loved to read instructions. Most importantly, Buddy became a child of his parents and a protector of his sister.

CHAPTER TWELVE

The Play of Death

Death is the constant but natural predator of the human ego; the hungry human ego is the constant predator of human happiness and wellbeing. Let's teach our children that death is a natural part of life that imparts freedom to our spirits.

My friend of almost fifty years told me the other day that she had experienced terror of dying. I asked her why. "You've done it so many times." (We are curious about living more than one life and try to find the humor.)

I have always been so fortunate to work with very smart and kind clients 99.9 percent of the thirty-three years in the field of mental health. So, the other day I was consulting with a parent, who had brought her child to therapy three years ago when her father died of cancer. She came back for a "tune-up." While we were discussing her particular metaphors, she asked me why her daughter might have a meltdown over one green pea showing up in her mac and cheese. She went on to explain that she as mom (being highly intelligent and logical) would stress out and demand to know why her daughter was crying. "It's just *one pea* in her entire macaroni and cheese. Whatever I say just makes it worse. How should I respond?"

I take lots of risks by doing what I do and saying what I say. "Well," I said, "you cannot talk to an upset, right-brain-flooded child out of her emotions; children are not little adults—not at all. You look at that pea in her mac and cheese and validate that it doesn't belong there; it is in the wrong place, and you know how upsetting it is when things are in the wrong place where they don't belong."

When I added that her father was in the wrong place, she got it. She exhaled. I added, "Sometimes children will use scraped knees, scary movies, bonked heads, et cetera, to grieve or cry about larger issues. Kids don't say, 'I'm so sad about my parent dying. I am going to cry right now.' They wait. When their body hurts, it's an opportunity to grieve."

This child used an old coin to ask, "Where is he?" (her father) by repeatedly losing and finding the coin in the playroom. She used her body to "splat!" and flip-flop while losing and finding the coin. This is a way children use their bodies as communication devices without really thinking about the form it takes. Her body movements and her words were all about her questions regarding her father's death and the effect her big emotions have on her body when an anniversary date comes by. She is a very bright child, but she cannot talk about her deepest inner feelings yet. So in the playroom she asked all her questions about death in play form, although she has asked her mother verbally, but the questions and answers just weren't satisfying to her. After only three sessions, her clinging behavior and separation anxiety decreased dramatically.

I'm well acquainted with death; this subject is predominant on the minds of many of the new kids. So many parents have reported their children screaming, "I want to die … kill myself … kill someone else. You hate me!" I was fairly unaware of suicide, even murder as a very young child. Nancy Drew just wasn't violent. I think the mystery of death has stalked me throughout my life.

One of my first memories of death brings me to a simple room, where my paternal grandfather's China-blue eyes met mine as he died. I was three, holding my father's hand. My grandmother sat in a heap of grief in their dark apartment in the shaded, tiny living room downstairs as he took his last breath.

When I was five, my two cousins (four and six years old) came to stay with us because their mother, the youngest of five of my mother's siblings, was having a baby. A week later the adults received the call. My aunt had died, and so had the baby. This news delivered to my young cousins was something like, "Your mother is dead. There is no baby sister." I literally watched as my younger cousin's spirit left his body; I saw this happen as we sat together on the cranberry-colored carpet of my parents' home. All I remember is adults with no heads, just legs and clothing ending at the neck. My year-older cousin just seemed to evaporate into the vapors of adult grief, cigarettes, and alcohol—oh, and church. As an adult, my younger cousin married two women who died before getting that unconscious belief to change. When I was six, my maternal grandfather went into the hospital located on one of the infamous Shelter Islands and never came out.

When I was nine years old, my faithful dog, Shadow, was brought to the house in a box on a rainy night after drowning in the convent guppy pool. Gene, the most loved school janitor, died a year later. When I was ten, my girlfriend entered the hospital to have her tonsils out, and she never to come out. The next time I saw her, she was laid out in a coffin. At nine, I was also told that my art teacher had died suddenly, and I would no longer be sketching in the golden fields of Long Island. After vandalizing my first (and only) house, I smoked my first cigarette at nine, snatched from one of my friend's packs, which he'd hid in a shed in back of their house. They had seven kids, and he was my dentist. The cigarettes were Chesterfields, unfiltered.

You get the picture; death and identity confusion has been a part of the tapestry of my life. Thirty people in my life have died. For someone who didn't live in a (declared) war zone I know about the many faces of death, about how children can respond and about how grieving in children and playing about death usually defy adult expectations about how it should look. We cannot comment, judge or sometimes even recognize the many forms of grieving in others.

I have played with children who have lost siblings, parents, grandparents, aunts, uncles, teachers, coaches, pets, and anyone else they loved through death. Some died of disease, some committed suicide, some died in an accident, and some were murdered. Like abuse, death is a tough one for children to process, but as a therapist, I find it easier because death is the great equalizer, and it will happen to everyone sooner or later. Naturally, it is overwhelmingly sad to lose a parent, a sibling, a caretaker, or a pet—anyone you care about or love. Losing one parent causes extreme separation anxiety regarding the surviving parent, and this is usually difficult for the surviving parent to cope with. The parent has his or her own grieving to do too. But I've seen children cope with death as an ongoing process of adjusting to loss; they do better emotionally than children who experience the effects of hateful, highly conflicted divorces—which are the worst, sometimes worse than death.

I know kids with parents who simply locked their children in a closet for hours so the parents could go out to a party at night. Emotional death is as real as physical death, and children clearly show these emotional losses—the eroding of human hope and fantasy and the beginning of the loss of innocence—in the playroom.

Children lose parents emotionally all the time. There they are, sitting at the dinner table, sharing their negativity, disinterest, and irritation while expecting their child to eat something dreaded (to the child). The parent is physically there but emotionally and psychically gone, like in the story of having tea with an alien and a werewolf. Sometimes emotional loss is harder than just outright losing someone; at least death is somehow cleaner. Sometimes it's easier to deal with a spanking than mean looks and name-calling or being shown how unimportant you are (invalidated, rejected) to your caretaker or parent, your loved one because it is a tangible, viable event that you know happened. Insidious energy violations are some of the most difficult to heal.

Invisible things have power, as Zack's story of momentum illustrates. These are the layers of momentum a four-year-old boy expressed on a multitude of levels. He created the perfect metaphor to describe his parents' friendly divorce. The undercurrent was wicked, and he was the conduit for that energy. It is indeed a type of death. But death holds the great mystery, and ultimately we can tell children only what will comfort them as children. And frankly, when we are dead and gone, what our bodies were becomes irrelevant; death is the great equalizer.

As part of the topic of death, the great stalker and teacher of humans, I want to point out that the children of today are not only tuned into death and dying. They deal with the fear of this truth at younger and younger ages and also threaten to kill either themselves or their friends when they are upset. Faith in something higher than us, perhaps even a divine part of ourselves, helps, and I support faith in life and being. When children ask me questions about death, I simply admit that I don't know what happens but that I know that what we believe is important. It maybe even influences our after-life journey as much as our perceptions shape our in-life experiences.

Children don't process the experience of death in the way adults may like to think they will. Tiny toy gravestones and skeletons may not be used as one would suspect, but almost always something is buried or missing, as one would suspect. Children are rarely taught that death is the inevitable result of living, and I think it would be most helpful to encourage children to think of death as a natural part of life. Of course, we miss the person who dies; our lives can fundamentally shift because of this loss, and most of all, we miss who we were with the person who is no longer physically present.

Much of children's play is acceptable and somewhat understood *unless and until* it points a finger at someone who didn't treat the child with respect and positive regard. Suddenly, play becomes something easy to dismiss and discard, and it isn't considered evidence of anything. And yet hundreds and hundreds of parents, witnessing their child's play, nod and drop jaws in recognition of their child's life situation as he or she illustrates it through his or her play.

The following soul story involves a six-year-old girl who overheard her mother cry out on the phone that her father was dead from suicide. The following are excerpts from a chapter I was asked to contribute to a college level play therapy textbook.[1]

Sadie was six and a half years old when I met her. Her story is an example of how young children process death and trauma, at least as it's happening in their lives.

Truly being with a trusted adult changes the way the entire experience of extreme loss is processed in the brain. Human beings need support; we are not built for total solitude.

Sadie's father hanged himself in prison while serving time for distribution of drugs. When Sadie's mother received the phone call, she cried aloud, "Oh my God! Denis hung himself!" and started freaking out. She went unconscious from the shock of the news and completely forgot that Sadie and her brother had witnessed their mother's breakdown upon receipt of the news that they had lost their father by his own hand.

Needless to say, Sadie is an intelligent child, with pretty good self-regulation skills, and remarkably the mother reported no pre-trauma incidents during the intake session. That's hard to believe, but it could be true.

Sadie's reaction to hearing the news of her father's sudden death by his own hand was one of denial and emotional numbing. She entered a terrifying labyrinth of churning with emotional turmoil; she had to find her way out of the darkness. That is why it's so important to play with young children for assessments. And here is the sticking point: Sadie played "scary father" in the playroom; her mother denied any frightening or out-of-order events related to Denis. *We, The Children* supports the idea that what lies in children's unconscious minds—or some truth they may hide from their caretakers—emerges in the right setting and is the truth of the matter.

Because it's the truth of the matter, the play should be respected.

So Mom was unaware of Sadie's "scary dad" memories, which came up later in therapy, but she understood that the suicide had complicated the actual trauma and death of her father. How does one explain this to a young child?

Sadie experienced some unusual symptoms, including forgetting the entire alphabet, which she had completely mastered and had been starting to read; sleep-walking; refusing to speak when angry; challenging all rules at school; as well as suggesting the possibility of experiencing hallucinations and other dissociative episodes.

Children feel deeply. For generations we have said, "Oh, they're just kids. They'll get over it." The truth is the opposite. Children *are* their feelings—and we, the adults, act out of those internalized feelings unless we have become very aware.

Sadie became obsessed with the alphabet. In her second session, it was clear that she didn't remember her first session. Her high need for (the illusion of) control showed in her use of a tiny red wagon and a shovel, showing by miniature shovelfuls that she couldn't take one more thing in her life.

The second session started the relearning and reaffirming of the alphabet as if she'd had an argument with words themselves and what those words could make you hear and then have to live. At first, Sadie recited, "A, B, C, D" and then started over. The alphabet might end at *D* if *D* is for Daddy— adults have to open their minds and hearts to see the metaphor presented by a child. Sadie wove a tale about having to relearn and rebuild trust in life and early childhood, relationships, herself, God, and so on—she sorted this out by also rearranging the magnetic letters or moving the letters in the big, rubber alphabet mat covering the playroom floor. This was a lot of work.

I just let her be. I understand that investigations seem to have a time limit, but then the case can drag on for years. So why not spend more time with the child who is the only other true witness to the events in his or her life?

Like I said, I just let her be, and little by little she reoriented herself and seemed to land back in her body. In her third session, somewhat satisfied with the arrangement of the ABCs (=childhood), she reported that "a man with no head" had come into her bedroom at night and stood at the side of her bed, scaring her terribly.

Then he was in the playroom, "the fake, invisible man." We all knew this man was her father, the projection of her loss of him. It had to be pretend to be approached. One of Sadie's coping mechanisms was to play that she was two years old again when her father was alive. In this role play, as directed by Sadie, she was the mommy, and I was assigned the role of the kid. This way I could reflect back to Sadie her own feelings of loss, thus validating her journey. As she reenacted the home dinner scene, complete with saying grace, she stated that the invisible man was staring at her. This "fake, invisible man" haunted Sadie, the playroom, and her home at night; real or imagined, we'll never know, but it was certainly real to Sadie. By her fourth sessions, it took her less time to get through the alphabet. Can you see the value of the alphabet as a metaphor for learning in childhood?

Her grasp of language and learning represented her ability to integrate this loss into her life. It wasn't until her tenth session that Sadie verbalized, "I feel mad about my dad." So asking young children to verbalize their trauma in a room full of strangers or with a police officer is asking for the cow to jump over the moon.

Then she pointed to the feelings poster (there are 24 human emotions illustrated on a laminate poster – children love to identify their feelings using this visual tool) and said, "He makes me sad too." Later, her mother told me that Sadie had slept all the way home and into the night until the next morning, undisturbed by sleepwalking or the invisible, headless man.

After five more sessions, Sadie left therapy. She stopped reciting the alphabet but wrote it out perfectly on the white board in perfect order. Sadie had integrated the loss of her father and shared, "He is my guardian angel now."

A check-in with her mother revealed that Sadie could now look at family albums, share feelings, and ask questions. She was freed from the headless, invisible man and could sleep peacefully in her own bed again.

Sadie's story, one of so many tales of trauma, demonstrates the power and speed with which young children can recover and begin to heal from a tragic and sudden loss. Although this type of grief is lifelong, Sadie grounded herself in reality and exorcised the haunting memories of her father's death.[2]

Here is Maddie's story of death and dying: When Maddie was nine months old, her father was diagnosed with cancer and placed in the hospital. Just after her second birthday, he died. When her mother brought her to the playroom, she felt that Maddie was following strange men around and trying to get their attention because she was searching for her daddy. Alarmed by Maddie's need for male attention and the bad dreams that pursued her child, Maddie's mom trusted that experiential play was the best path for Maddie to process. Maddie was the youngest of two girls; the family moved three times since her father's death. Maddie talked about her father's death incessantly; this habit was concerning and an almost constant cry for need of some kind of resolution.

Adults generally try to help children verbally express about the death they endured. In Maddie's case, we wanted to direct her thoughts back to life. At night she prayed, "Thank God for Daddy. God, can you give him back? It's okay if you can't; you must need him too [as nanny reported to me]."

Here is another point: the day of her third session was the third anniversary of her father's death, and she played "lost kids and lost kitties."

This is another behavior parents misunderstand and overlook unless it becomes the child's main operating system: turning into and playing animals as a way of containing wild feelings and distancing himself or herself from human emotions.

Next time she made a complete family of cows. Slowly, she gained control over the feelings she churned with into acceptance. She tried to hide the death of her father from everyone, mostly herself. After she could acknowledge every feeling on the feelings chart (about twenty-four feelings), she declared herself "happy." At home, her mother reported the cessation of nightmares. She was less clingy and whiny, and she made only the occasional mention of death; she also slept safely in her own bed.

During her final sessions, Maddie cleared the playroom of "ghosts" (bad memories or fears) and created a cow family in the sandbox with the mother in the lead, her older sister next, and she behind her sister, with "Dad behind them." In this powerful metaphor of acceptance, Maddie found her rightful place in the family and showed she was putting the death of her father behind them.

A Little Bit More

Some of these stories are old stories from many years ago. As I rewrite them, I'm again persuaded of the importance of paying more attention to what children are playing if you really want to get to know and understand their experiences. It seems that as long as there are no accusations of abuse involved, the play themes and brilliant metaphors are fairly easy to see and comprehend, even appreciate, for their accuracy.

But what is true is true on all levels. What remains true is that children are dependent on adults to regain their balance when life goes upside down. Young children have even less capacity to understand death and dying, regain control over their anxiety and separation issues, and may go intensely seeking the deceased person. The gift of a playroom and an adult who gets it is that this situation allows even very young children to express themselves and process the incomprehensible.

As an adult who truly commits to listening to children's stories, which is all we ever really have, our stories, there are the healers who rediscover the essence of humanity in each child's story. Faith in another's story is the key to humanity's ability to believe strongly and move out of programming and into our hearts.

Whoever tells the story holds power over the patient and attentive listener. Parenting and interacting with children are a lot like storytelling. Adults are always "talking story" to children. "I believe you; I don't believe you; not true, true. You dreamed it, made it up—your mother made you say that. You're a good child; you're a bad child, wonderful—horrible!" The story we grow up with, the one we tell ourselves about ourselves evolves from the twists and turns on our journey. Most importantly, the story your child tells himself or herself, truth or lies, is the one he or she believes.

This is the point.

Conclusion: Rethinking Thoughts, Words, and Deeds

Life is precious, no matter how we perceive it, and it is up to grown-ups to believe this. I'll tell you why. Too many parents hear these words: "I want to die." "I thought about killing my little sister; she gets all the attention." "I don't want to live." Children are living in a culture of fear, but we have the power to create a culture of love by recognizing and admitting that we are all an expression of humanity and whatever amazing force created us and frankly that we are all in the same boat on this planet. Although it appears that this boat is sinking, we can throw a life preserver to the children by joining with them at the deeper levels of both seen and unseen dimensions of reality.

For generations adults have proclaimed that "they are kids; they will get over it." And yes, most of us get over it, sort of. But what is true is that children weep soulfully, and from their breaking hearts, they express their anger passionately and love unconditionally. The most forgiving heart is that of a little child. Most children still get to experience the world as their laboratory, a magical wonderland to explore and learn to interpret in a happy and exciting way. But it seems that with the emphasis on technology, children are simply exposed to too much information too soon, and they need help to express and process their feelings and experiences more than ever before.

No matter how the clay of our most formative years (they are all formative years due to the brain's elasticity) brought us and taught us, those years were the one time we were our true and authentic selves. For most adults, childhood was all just once-upon-a-time experienced as a fairy tale, a horror story or some story in-between. We forgot; now, we need to remember our formative years and the unconscious force these experiences control our adult lives to develop self-compassion and return to our original selves.

Way back in April 2001, an eleven-year-old boy named Gregory announced to the world, "I believe that through compassion, understanding, and moral character development, we can achieve a nonviolent society that cares for the needs of others."

As we, the adults, embark on this journey backward across an invisible but energetically tangible bridge linking the child's world with the adult word, a wealth of adventure and treasure awaits us. I say, let's join the Gregories of this world and become not only their teachers but also their students.

Like all of us, the new kids thrive on healthy connection with others; none of us can accomplish this healing alone.

Mindfulness has become an almost annoying word, like organic but represent the lesser of evils. But humans have to choose. Choose wisely between the opposites and strive for balance, connection and integration of our duality.

CHAPTER THIRTEEN

The Children's Bill of Rights

The Children's Bill of Rights as presented here is, in part, the invention of my mind. I have witnessed too many children suffering because of adult behaviors and decisions. 2016 may be the year to consider an actual legal document that would ensure children's rights in the real world and not just on websites and books.

2016 and Forward: I recommend that children be granted basic human and political rights, that children's verbal and nonverbal testimony be considered as vital and viable testimony to be considered by child interviewers, courts, attorneys, guardians, teachers, and other adults making life-altering decisions for children. I believe that their testimony should be considered true and legitimate until proved otherwise.

All children have the right not to be bullied and to be protected while enjoying their right to a public education. Federal law protects the rights of students with disabilities to be recognized, but federal law has yet to recognize the right of all students from bullying. A law that recognizes this right for all children would provide a civil rights protection to public education. Additionally, we might benefit as a society to provide treatment for the bullies themselves as well as recognizing the long term and dangerous outcomes of bullying.

It is statistically true, according to *The Monitor on Psychology*, that preschool children are over diagnosed with "disorders" and overmedicated.[1] When will we learn that the environment isn't working for the children—at least most of the ones who act out?

Although many state and federal agencies work hard to create laws to protect children, the reality of court and other processes may tell a significantly different story.

House Bill 2451: State of Washington, 63rd Legislature in the 2014 Regular Session states, "The American Psychological Association's task force on appropriate therapeutic responses to sexual orientation issued a report in 2009 concluding that sexual orientation change efforts can pose critical health risks to lesbian, gay, and bisexual people, including suicidal thoughts and many other dangers … Is not a disease, disorder, illness, deficiency, or shortcoming. Is our concept of what it means to be human simply changing?

1998: Special Concerns of Children Committee, March 1998 (Divorce and Kids' Rights)

1996: Children from seven countries and three continents communicated with each other over the Internet, agreed on a list of natural and basic rights of children all over the world, and attempted to ratify them; this information is easily obtained by simply typing in "Children's Rights" at Google.com.

1990: The Child Abuse Protection Act of 1990 passed by Congress allows children to submit victim impact statements in a manner "commensurate with their age and cognitive development." Some states are following the federal government's lead by allowing children to submit hand-drawn pictures or letters to the sentencing court.

1975: Education of All Handicapped Children Act (revised in 1990) Individuals with Disabilities Education Act (IDEA)

1980's: The discovery of child sexual abuse

1979–1983: The creation of the National Center for Child Abuse and Neglect

1961: The discovery of child abuse

1959: The first written document on the rights of the child[2]

This list comprises some facts and some hopes and dreams for children.

Each child's story represents the hero's journey replete with struggles to recover some measure of dignity and worth, and to understand, cope with, and impact the adult world. By the time children enter a therapeutic playroom, they have lost their sense of dignity and worth, and indeed have suffered some level of a soul murder or damage to the essential self. Eggs can be unscrambled as a child's inner journey takes him or her from victim to the hero of his or her story. Children get to drop the baggage as it collects and especially so when adult in their lives when remembering the language of childhood, support them. Given the opportunity, they can heal their lives. Processing events as they occur is fundamentally different than carrying that baggage around for twenty, thirty and more years. When their story is dismissed as merely child's play, vitally important information is often overlooked in life-altering court decisions or, worse, by the therapist, interviewer, or parent.

I think it's time for the legal system and other systems to expand their view when confronted with cases involving young kids and allegations of invasive behaviors. Yes, sure, kids make up stories that aren't true. They can be coached, threatened, or bribed into making false accusations; but prisons are full of innocent people who got locked up by lying adults who did the same thing, and most are not denied the right to true representation in court or anywhere else. It is the old worn-out systems, fraught with assumptions and fears, that are changing, and nothing can stop this from happening.

(And no, I don't think very many angry teens have the right to sue the adults in their lives; this isn't about that kind of consideration.) This is about what we know to be true. Did researchers really have to deprive those little monkeys of their mothers to find out they would go insane without them? Or do they do slightly better with the wire and cloth mother while devoid of the warmth and softness of their natural mother? Didn't we already know that? Didn't we already know that when an infant cries, it needs our attention? Didn't we already know that screaming in distress for any undue amount of time will not strengthen the character of an infant or toddler? Did we need fifty years of research to prove that, in most cases, breast milk is superior to formula? As the kids would exclaim, "Come on!"

I can hear protests to what this type of thinking produces, and to a point I agree. But consider the stories themselves as proof of children's ability to communicate.

We, as a species, have sold out to our basest urges and have conditioned, unconscious prejudices. This may not be the work of the devil, and I sincerely doubt that it is, but it is the work the ego. We are witnessing an extremely aware generation of creative problem solvers. By opening to their inner knowing to connect deeply with all we have become as human beings, they provide for all of us what the child advocates have to say. The thing is, the kids are us—and in the near future, they are our leaders. What we do to children we do to ourselves. What we teach our children we become as humans. When will we wake up?

In the Western world, we have more insidious means of undermining children than in India, where advocates fight to free child laborers. In Syria children are used as human shields, and in other places (Pakistan, Iraq, and so forth) they are targets for drone attacks. If we look at the world, it seems that the healthiest places work hard to raise healthy children with balanced egos. Since the feedback we get from others as children forms children's self-concepts, imagine the imprint of being ignored by a hardworking judge. Imagine being kept awake at night because of lack of recognition regarding reasonable doubt against the offending adult in child cases. Imagine if the judge says a child has to go hang out with someone who has hurt him or her because, well, that person doesn't even know the child. Not considering his or her non-verbal language as testimony may lead to a unfair trial and a dangerous decision.

Fortunately, some judges are parents too and the ones who often consider a child's words and play as a valid form of testimony, if a credible adult presents them. Children deserve a vote regarding the degree of relationship with a possibly harmful adult when there is reasonable doubt as to the motives of the parent, caretaker, or guardian. They are sometimes amazingly given a choice; I have seen this happen—not often, but it does happen.

Play therapy done well nurtures a child's ego and his or her spirit; the relationship and the process transcend logic because, although we try to apply logic to development, development is full of surprises. What isn't surprising and hasn't changed is the need to progress through and master each stage of development on every level, whether it belongs to the world of spirit, body, mind, or soul.

Humans can only pretend to be somewhere they're not in the reality of social, emotional, and spiritual development. Sooner or later the poser's façade breaks down one way or another.

I had a friend growing up, a good Irish Catholic girl. She got in with some bad guys with bad drugs and had a complete nervous breakdown. Her beauty and intelligence as well as her body returned to the developmental stage of about twelve years old. Basically, she never came back, and the loss of her was worse than death itself. The point is the power of the mind, the power of the unconscious and where we truly reside inside. Danger follows this level of denial, as too many adults sleepwalk through life.

The human ego and the human spirit don't share the same thought system, in fact; the thought systems are opposite, just as our animal natures and our divine natures are opposites and have opposite goals. Our spiritual goal is to heal and create; our ego's goal is to consume and devour the planet. Beware! According to *A Course in Miracles,* the ego's creed is "seek and don't find."

The truly therapeutic playroom is designed to help children sort out their experiences and feelings, and create a healthy and balanced ego for themselves, which means feeling good about who they are in a solid and clean way, not distorted by delusions of being bad or perfect but embracing what it means to be human.

I'm not sure the metaphor of holding the world in the palm of our hands was ever referring to cell phones. Believe it or not, adults who are mesmerized by their phones can help create feelings of separation and abandonment in the child sitting helplessly next to them. Mainly, although technology connects, it also teaches a powerful lesson of separation in the moment—me in my world, you in yours.

Kids and teens may abandon Face Book when they see their aunties, uncles, or parents on there; and they switch to Instagram or the next new social media channel. I'm not sure we can keep up with them. What we need to do is emphasize eye contact with children and find a balance between freedom and privacy for kids. The website below offers ideas on how to be fair to both the adult (who usually pays for the technology) and the child who needs both protection and privacy.

(Youth Internet Safety Task Force/WA State Office of Attorney @ www.atg.wa.gov/VISTF.aspx)

A long time ago, an unknown author wrote this poem:

> I tried to teach my child with books,
> She gave me only puzzled looks,
> They passed her by often unheard.
> Despairingly, I turned aside
> How shall I teach my child? I cried.
> Into my hand she put the key.
> Come, she said, play with me.

Play is a positive experience; a brilliant architect of the brain, mind body and soul.

References

Introduction

[1] "Self-Directed Violence" (lecture, UW Medical School of Medicine and Seattle Children's Hospital, Bellingham, WA, May 1, 2015).

[2] This is part fiction, part fact; it was given to me sixteen years ago while this child was in therapy. Names, dates, gender, and location have been changed to protect any association with anyone at anytime.

Chapter One

* This section is not a quote from any source other than the author's mind.

[1] Virginia Axline, *Dibs in Search of Self, Play Therapy* (Ballantine Books, New York, 1980). Pages 195-`96. This book is so old it's yellow, but the message has yet to be fully heard and incorporated into our thinking about children.

[2] Play therapy research and articles: http://www.apa.org/pubs/journals/pla. This research shows that children's play is an accurate reflection of their experience.

[3] Erick Erikson/Psychosocial Stages/Simply Psychology; http://www.simplypsychology.org/Erik -Erickson-html

Chapter Two

1 Carol and Byron Norton, *Reaching Children through Play Therapy: An Experiential Approach,* p. 2-45, The Publishing Cooperative, 1836 Blake Street, Denver, CO,1997).

2 The Holy Bible, 1 Corinthians 13:11, King James Version

Chapter Three

1 Robert Louis Stevensen, *The Strange Case of Dr. Jekyll and Mr. Hyde,* first published around 1886.

2 *The Children's Bill of Rights*, Special Concerns Committee, March 1998. I found this on the Internet: http://www.childrensrights.com *When Parents Are Not Together*

3 Rumi (poem from a 2014 calendar)

Chapter Four

1 These are excerpts from a conversation with seven-year-old girl many years ago in Colorado. Names and other identifying features have either been omitted or changed to protect identities.

2 Information regarding child sexual abuse, court, and other effects: http://www.childabusesolutions.com. Plus see great article published by Association for Counselor Education and Supervision Conference, October 11–14, Columbus, Ohio 2007 or www.safehorizons.org/page/child-abuse-get-help-14.html

Clare Haynes-Seman and David Baumgarten, *Children Speak for Themselves: Using the Kempe Interactional Assessment to Evaluate Allegations of Parent-Child Sexual Abuse* (Brunner/Mazel, 1994).

3 Jim B. Tucker, *Return to Life: Extraordinary Cases of Children Who Remember Past Lives* (St. Martin's Press, 2013, "The Third James, p 63 -87.

Chapter Five

1 Morning Edition, North West Public Radio—NPR—January, 2015.

2 http://www.change.org/petitions/stop-the-victimization-of-mothers-reporting-sexual-abuse.

3 M. Scott Peck, M.D., *People of the Lie: The Hope for Healing Human Evil, p.43,* (Simon & Schuster Building, 1230 Avenue of the Americas, New York, New York, 10020, 1983).

4 http://www.childabusesoltutions.com.

5 The National Child Abuse and Neglect Data Systems (NCANDS), which contains child protective service data.

6 *The Child Maltreatment 2006 Report*, Darkness to Light, 2001–2005 (NCANDS data).

Chapter Six

1 Provided by the author: I received this information over a decade ago from a child I call Jewel. I met her when the wave of realization was washing over me about the seeming simultaneous evolution of childhood as well as its end.

Chapter Ten

1 North West Public Radio, Morning Edition, July 2015, Bellingham, WA.

2 Nicolas Riccardi, "Rights Case Ruling Favors Colorado Transgender Girl," Associated Press, June 24, 2013.

3 For more beautiful information regarding the gender-fluid child, read Stephanie Brill and Rachel Pepper, *The Transgender Child: A Handbook for Families and Professionals* (Cleis Press, 2008) and Lori Duron, *Raising My Rainbow* (Broadway Books, 3013).

Chapter Thirteen

1 *The Monitor on Psychology* 46, no 7, p. 64, (July/August 2015).

2 The Children's Bill of Rights was compiled from a variety of sources and referenced, to the best of my knowledge, within the text. See http://www.childrensbillofrights.org.

www.ingramcontent.com/pod-product-compliance
Lightning Source LLC
Chambersburg PA
CBHW020518290526
45786CB00002B/665

* 9 7 8 1 5 0 4 3 4 5 7 5 0 *